CW00434464

# GLEN FESHIE

## The History and Archaeology of a Highland Glen

By Meryl M Marshall

Published by the North of Scotland Archaeological Society

Printed by A4 Design & Print Ltd, Inverness

## Preface

Glen Feshie is one of the most beautiful places in the Cairngorm National Park, iconic for its ancient pine forests, towering mountains and sparkling waterfalls, famous for its black grouse, crossbills and deer. Wild though it is, however, like everywhere in the Highlands, it is steeped in history: it is the interaction between nature and people that makes it so interesting. This excellent short book tells it all, from the old shieling systems and the deserted farmtouns high in the glen once growing grain (it seems incredible now), to the days of the nineteenth century deer stalkers. Particularly fascinating are the high jinks of the Duchess of Bedford, holding parties in her "huts" with her friend Sir Edwin Landseer and other guests, playing at turning their backs on civilisation. It is all a far cry from the usual idea of Victorians as prim and proper. There are lots of illustrations - maps, archaeological drawings, photographs, paintings, some contrasting what Landseer saw with the same scene today. What a useful book!

T. C. Smout.
Historiographer Royal in Scotland
October 2005


**Enjoy Scotland's outdoors responsibly**

Everyone has the right to be on most land and inland water providing they act responsibly. Your access rights and responsibilities are explained fully in the Scottish Outdoor Access Code.

Whether you're in the outdoors or managing the outdoors, the key things are to:

- **take responsibility for your own actions**
- **respect the interests of other people**
- **care for the environment.**

Visit **outdooraccess-scotland.com** or contact your local Scottish Natural Heritage office.

## Introduction to First Edition

Glen Feshie has been one of my favourite places for many years. I first visited the area in 1964 and have since spent many happy hours exploring the glen. Following completion of the Certificate of Field Archaeology through Aberdeen University in 1998, it seemed an obvious target to focus my attention on. I embarked on a project, the aim of which was to survey and record the archaeology of the glen south of the settlement of Tolvah, and of the Allt Fhearnasdail. This would appear to be a huge task as it involves many square kilometres of heathery upland and mountains with an altitude of 300m to 1,200m. The actual area prospected was about 20 square kilometres. Inevitably most of the archaeology was found along the valley floor. The project was to take me 4 years and the final report was produced in October 2003.

During the historical research for the project I investigated documents from both primary and secondary sources. Rentals and correspondence of the Mackintosh of Mackintosh family in the National Archive of Scotland and the Edward Ellice Papers in the National Library of Scotland were explored, as were the census records, Roy's Military Survey, c1750, and the Thomson map of 1830. There are a number of accounts of life in the early 19th century, when the glen was developed as a sporting estate. William Collie, who spent his early days working for the estate during this time, wrote his memoirs in later life and gives an insight into a childhood and a life in the employment of the "sporting fraternity". There are contemporary accounts of some of the guests who were invited to join the shooting parties in the glen. I make no excuse for quoting these extensively, as I feel they give a flavour of the times, however the Highlands were viewed in a very romantic light during this time and the language and descriptions seem "over the top" today. Last, but not least, there is the work of the Victorian painter Sir Edwin Landseer who derived much inspiration from the glen. All the drawings and paintings in the book are painted by Landseer unless otherwise stated, it must however be remembered that his was the romantic view in vogue at the time. In fact Landseer, through his paintings, almost certainly added to the romantic image of the Highlands. A major exhibition of his work, "The Monarch of the Glen - Landseer in the Highlands", at the National Galleries of Scotland in the summer of 2005 figured many paintings of Glen Feshie.

I would like to acknowledge the help received in producing this book; to members of the North of Scotland Archaeological Society for undertaking survey and excavation work, to Kate Doyle who helped me with some of the research in Edinburgh, to George Dixon, Norman Newton and last but not least to the Glen Feshie Estate and Thomas Macdonnell. This publication is principally concerned with the history and archaeology of that part of the glen which was the subject of the survey ie. south of Tolvah. Many people have shown interest in the project and it seemed that the best way to share the information was through a publication.

Meryl M. Marshall, October 2005

## Introduction to Second Edition

Inevitably new material has come to light since publication of the First Edition of the book. The 19th century photographs of AM Urquhart were perhaps the most exciting, but others too, of the bothy at Ruigh Aiteachan in the 1930s and the remains of the Landseer frescoes on the chimney piece also in the 1930s - my thanks to Pete Moore for these. I have been able to do more research in the Macpherson Grant of Ballindalloch papers enabling a more balanced history of settlement in the glen and I would like to thank Mr and Mrs Russell for their help. More information has come to light on the shielings in the glen, through the Macpherson Grant papers and through David Taylor, who carried out research into the shielings of neighbouring Glen Tromie. I am very grateful to him for allowing me to include some of his findings and also to Mary Mackenzie for her work on emigration from Glen Feshie and its neighbourhood. I have included a chapter on the Duchess of Gordon's farmstead at Kinrara which undoubtedly provided the inspiration for Duchess of Bedford's settlement in Glen Feshie and I have finished off by bringing the glen into the 20th Century with a piece on the military training during WW2, in this I appreciate the information given to me by a former resident at the time.

The spate of the River Feshie in September 2009 not only took away the bridge at Carnachuin but also the building that we had excavated in 2004-2005. Proof if proof was needed, of the powerful nature of the weather and the river in the glen.

MMM, February 2013

## And from NOSAS

Following the very successful reception of the first edition of this book, which was quickly sold out, it is my pleasure to welcome this second edition. It includes some new pictures and photographs, new documentary research and also new information bringing the glen into the 21st century. In 2007 our Glen Feshie project, which included the survey and excavation work as well as the book, was joint winner of the Council for British Archaeology's Marsh Community Award, an award made to encourage local communities to research the past around them and to convey a passion for our cultural heritage to future generations. This award was a significant feather in our cap and we were very proud to receive it. Since its formation in 1999 NOSAS has gone from strength to strength and today has a membership of over 100. We all share the same avid enthusiasm for archaeology and are involved in a variety of activities from the surveying, recording and excavation of sites to their conservation, presentation and interpretation. We feel we make a significant contribution to the awareness of our cultural heritage. By publishing this work, NOSAS fulfills its objectives of furthering the study of archaeology in the North of Scotland and promoting that interest to a wider audience. We wholeheartedly commend it to the reader. Enjoy!

Anne Coombs, NOSAS Chairperson, February 2013

# Contents

## Placenames of Glen Feshie

The spelling of placenames throughout this book may vary according to the source and the period from which the name originates.

*Feshie* - is thought to mean "fairy water" from the gaelic "feith sithean"

*Dalnavert* - from "Dail-an-bheart" meaning "dale of the grave or trench"

*Fhearnasdail* - the first part "fearna" means alder tree, the second part "dail" is from the Norse "dal" meaning valley. A variation of the same element, "stil", is found in the settlement names of Corarnstilmore and Corarnstilbeg

*Baileguish* - "township of the pine trees"

*Tolvah* - "hole of the drowning"

*Drumcaillich* - "ridge of the old woman"

*Achlean* - "broad field"

*Stronetoper* - "hillside of the well"

*Achleum/Achleum-a-choid* - "field of the leap"

*Allt Fhearnagan* - "stream of the alder trees"

*Coire Garbhlach* - "corrie of the rugged place"

*Righ na Bruach* - "stretch or shieling of the bank, border or edge"

*Ruigh Aiteachain* - "stretch or shieling of the junipers"

*Ruigh Fionntaig* - "stretch or shieling of the fair stream"

*Slochd Beag* - "smaller hollow"

# 1. Setting the Geographical and Historical Scene

The River Feshie is a tributary of the River Spey which flows through the area known as Badenoch to the north of the Cairngorm Mountains. The Feshie rises in the hills to the southwest of the Cairngorm Mountains, close to the boundary of the Atholl and Mar Estates, and flows northeast for 6 kilometres before turning abruptly to the northwest at the watershed with the Geldie Water. This point is significant in that it is a prime example of "river capture"; the uppermost part of the river, having once flowed eastward towards the Geldie, now turns back on itself to drain in the opposite direction. In its upper half the river runs through barren, exposed mountain country; no habitation and only the remains of a few shielings are to be found. The lower northern half of the glen is a glaciated U-shape with a flat valley floor and steep heathery hillsides which rise steeply on the east side to form the plateau of the Cairngorm Mountains. Inevitably these mountains attract the rough weather from the west; Glen Feshie is renowned for its wet and windy weather and the river is prone to flash flooding making its course well braided in places. Several tributaries have deposited small fertile fluvial outwashes on the valley floor; this inevitably, is where man has left his mark.

Today there are only two permanently occupied settlements in Glen Feshie south of Tolvah; Carnachuin, the base for the Glenfeshie estate, and Achlean, a small pastoral farm of mixed cattle and sheep. The glen appears largely deserted. But it has not always been so empty; there is evidence of human activity stretching back 400 years. This book tells the story of the glen over these centuries, describing the historical events and relating them to some of the archaeological sites which are seen today.

Much of the glen in the original archaeological survey is part of the Glenfeshie Estate which is currently managed with conservation and regeneration of the indigenous Caledonian pine forest and the natural habitats as the main objectives. The estate is no longer maintained as a sporting estate but control of deer numbers may be carried out throughout the year. The glen is much loved and much frequented by hill walkers, bikers and nature lovers. Public access by car on the east side of the river is as far as Achlean, where there is a large car park, and on the west side of the river as far as Tolvah, after which a private estate road (no unauthorised vehicles) traverses the glen to Carnachuin.

The route following Glen Feshie and Glen Geldie has been a route through the Grampian Mountains for many hundreds of years. It links Badenoch in the north to Blair Atholl and Braemar in the southeast. Two further early routes a short distance to the west, "Comyn's Route" and the "Minigaig Pass", were the main north-south routes prior to the construction of the Wade road over the Drumochter Pass in 1730. In early times travellers from the south heading for the northeast probably descended Glen Feshie from the summit of the Minigaig Pass. Documents refer to King Edward III's army marching from Perth to Lochindorb "through Blair Atholl, Glen Feshie and Strathspey" in their attempt to subdue Scots resistance during the Second War of Scottish Independence in 1336. Over the years there have been several proposals for the construction of a road through the glen but none has come to fruition. A map produced by Avery in 1735 shows the line of a proposed route "from Ruthven in Badenoch to Braemar". This road was intended as part of the scheme to link the government garrisons which controlled the Highlands following the 1715 rebellion. In 1828 the Commissioners for Highland Roads and Bridges considered the Glen Feshie - Glen Geldie route as one of the options for a new north-south road and even in 1953, a road through the glen to Braemar was considered.

In 1452 the forests of Badenoch and Lochaber had been gifted to the Earl of Huntly *(later Duke of Gordon)* for services to King James II at the battle of Brechin. The section of the "Forest of Glenfeshie" east of the River Feshie was held in feu from the Duke of Gordon by Lachlan Mackintosh of Mackintosh, Chief of the Clan and sometimes known as "the Mackintosh". The part west of the river was held by Macpherson of Invereshie. Scrope writes the following, attributing his information to Cluny McPherson, chief of Clan Chattan:

> The Earls of Huntly possessed in former times by far the most extensive range of hills and deer forests in Great Britain; they commenced at Ben Avon in Banff-shire and terminated at Ben Nevis, a distance of seventy miles. This immense tract of land was divided into seven distinct portions, each of which was given in charge to the most influential gentleman in its neighbourhood. Braefeshie formed one of these portions, its extent was 15 square miles *(the old Scots mile varied but was generally longer than the English mile)* (Scrope, 1883).

In 1568 the Earl of Huntly gave a charter of the lands of Dalnavert and South Kinrara *(now known as Inshriach)*, to Lachlan Mackintosh as compensation for the beheading of his father, William Mackintosh, whilst on a social call in 1550. Dalnavert and South Kinrara were sometimes referred to as "the Davochs of the Head" - perhaps because of this connection! These lands were leased to the family of Shaw in c1620 and remained with them until the early 19th century when the male line died out.

Angus Macpherson was the first to possess the Invereshie estates on the west side of the River Feshie. In 1637, he was granted a "charter of few *(sic)* farme" by George, Marquis of Huntly, for "the lands of Invereshie, Culteloid *(now Ballintean)* and Coirarnsdalemore" (NAS GD 44/28/7/1/1). The lands were sold to Macpherson of Dalraddie c1694 and his successor assumed the name Invereshie. He was succeeded by his son George, who in 1731 married Grace, daughter of Colonel William Grant of Ballindalloch. Their son, William, succeeded but died unmarried in 1812 and was followed by his nephew George, born in 1781. In 1806 George inherited the estate of Ballindalloch and assumed the surname Grant. He was made a Baronet in 1838 and was MP for Sutherland from 1830 to 1846. He was:

> shrewd, ambitious and determined, party and men were made subservient to his wishes, and he was steadily successful. He bought up at great expense all the ridiculous but burdensome stipulations in his Gordon charters, finally acquiring not only the freehold of Invereshie, but the lands of Invertromie, and also a great slice of the Gordon Kingussie lands. (Fraser Mackintosh, 1863).

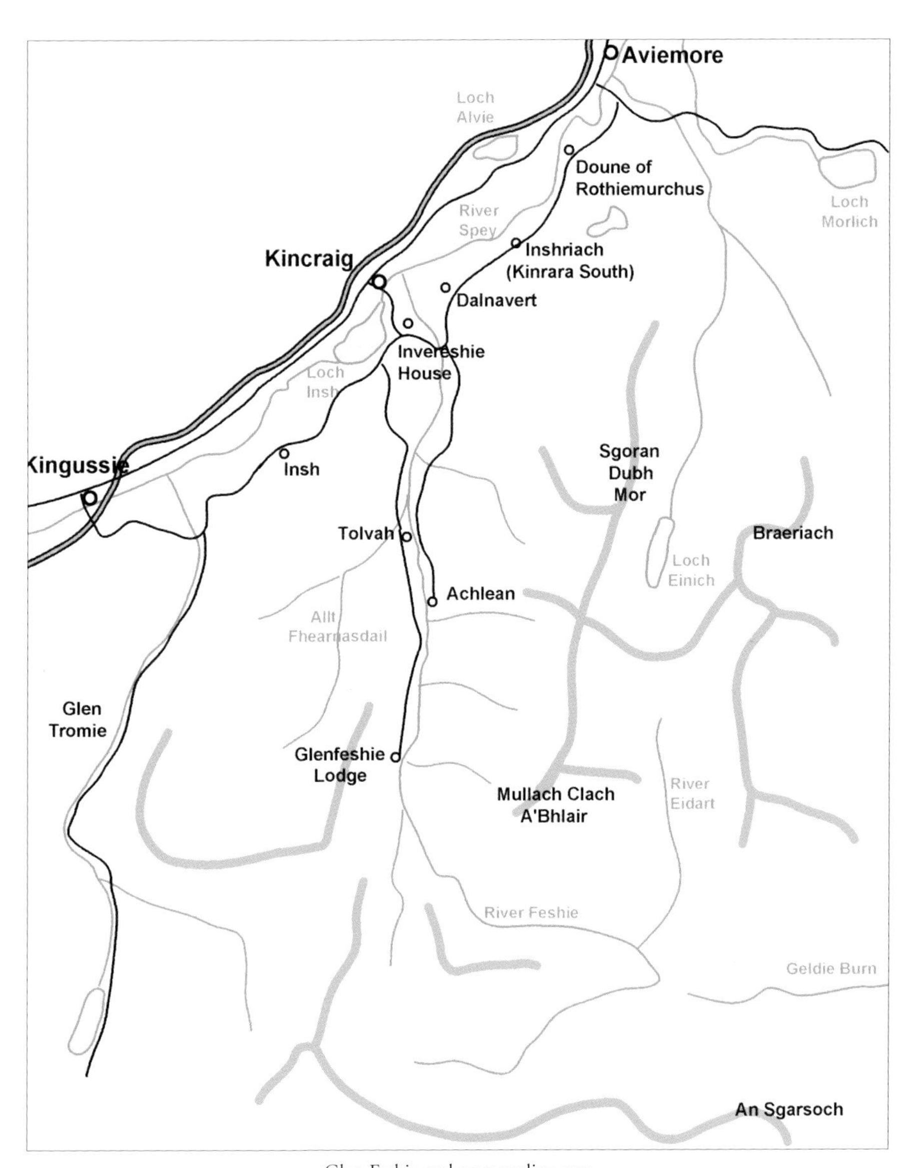


Glen Feshie and surrounding area

Upper Glen Feshie and Ruigh Fionntaig, 2005

*Glenfishie*, c1830-1835 - Courtesy of Simon C Dickinson Ltd

In the early half of the 19th century the Gordon family, like many of the old order of Highland families experienced financial problems. The estate was heavily in debt and George Gordon, the 5th and last Duke of Gordon, was obliged to sell many of his Badenoch properties. George Macpherson Grant purchased the west part of Glen Feshie in 1816 and was particularly active in leasing it as a sporting estate. In 1873 the Macpherson Grants gained control of the whole of the glen by leasing the east bank of the Feshie from "the Mackintosh". It was a most desirable shooting estate and was let over the next period to various shooting tenants at steadily increasing rents. In 1925 the east bank of the river was purchased bringing the whole of the upper glen under one ownership.

The glen and the Lodge were requisitioned by the army during World War II and used as a military training ground between 1942 and 1946. Since 1967 the estate has changed hands several times and is now owned by a Danish industrialist. It is recognized as being of significant importance ecologically with rare habitats for flora and fauna and is being managed sympathetically.

Today Glen Feshie is in the parish of Alvie, but prior to 1931 only the east bank of the River Feshie was in this parish; the west bank was part of the quoad sacra parish of Insh, which had been separated from Kingussie parish in 1833. In 1931 Insh and Alvie parishes were joined together and given the name of the latter.

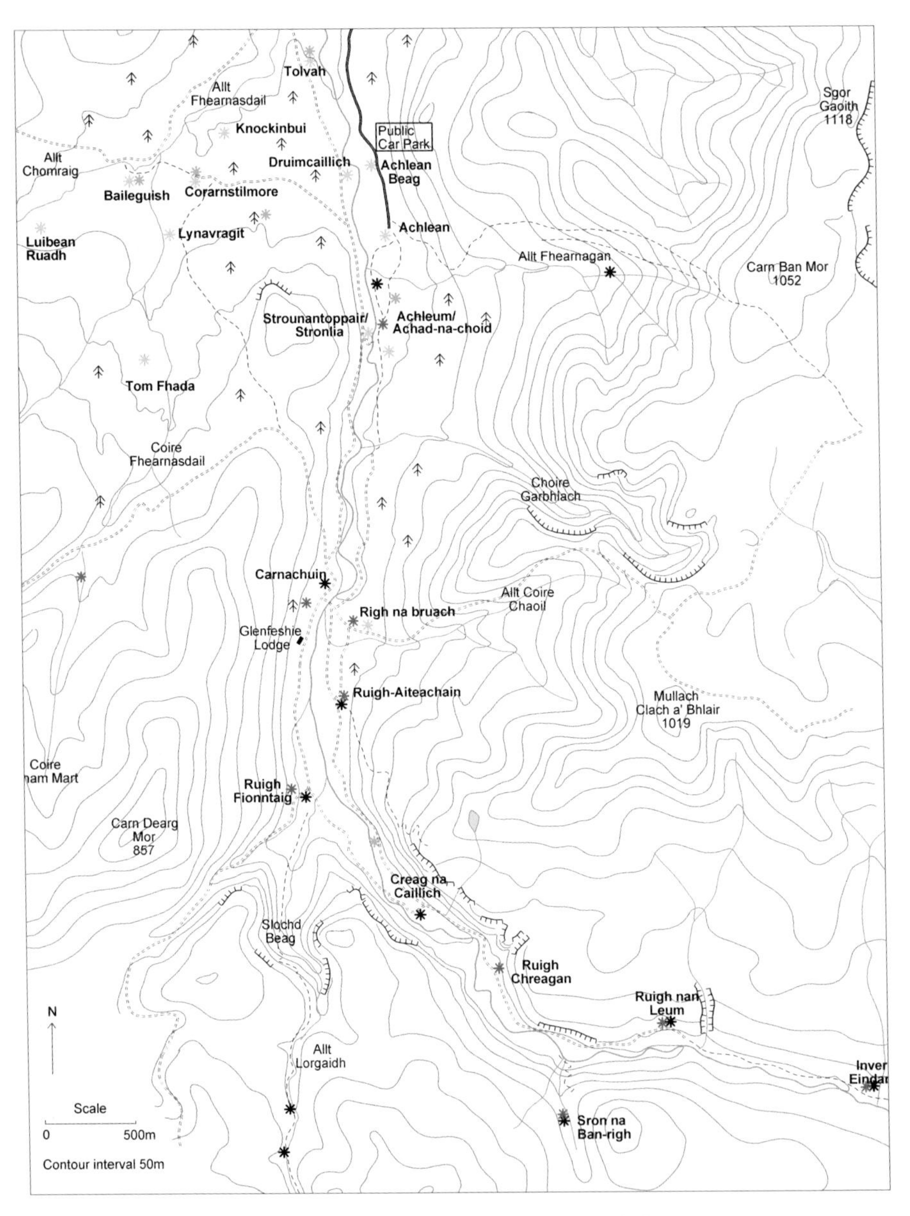


**Glen Feshie - location of archaeological sites**

* shieling sites * townships * sheepfarming sites * sites of sporting period

## 2. Shielings and Townships – the Pre-improvement Cattle Period

The "Forrest of Glenfishie" is mentioned in an Act of Parliament of 1685. Although regarded as a hunting forest at this time, no reference to it being used as such was found and Scrope writes:

> The whole of this vast tract *(the land between Ben Avon and Ben Nevis)* was not solely appropriate for breeding deer, for tenants were allowed to erect shielings in the confines of the forest and their cattle were permitted to pasture as far as they chose during the day, but they were bound to bring them back to the shielings in the evenings; and such as were left in the forest over night were liable to be poinded. These regulations answered very well between Huntly and his tenants, but they made an opening for small proprietors, who held in fee *(feu)* from the Gordon family, to make encroachments, and in course of time to acquire a property to which they had not the smallest legal title. In other respects rights were rigidly adhered to, for the old forest laws, which were exceedingly severe, were enforced to the utmost in this district; mutilation and even death were resorted to for depredations committed in the forest ..........No alteration took place in these forests till after the Rebellion of 1745 when the whole was let for grazing.........in consequence of cattle being admitted to summer grazing the present number of deer is not great (Scrope, 1883)

Until the end of the 18th century the rearing of black cattle was the mainstay of Highland subsistence and economy. Milk, butter, cheese and meat provided food for the Highlander, hides contributed towards his comfort and clothing and butter and cheese paid his rent "in kind". Later there was a demand from the growing population centres of the south for meat and export of the cattle to satisfy this demand provided much needed revenue.

At this time the Highlanders lived in townships, with each tenant or family having their own house but sharing resources with the other tenants. A township comprised a cluster of buildings, adjacent arable land or "infield" and a few enclosures, all of which were surrounded by a head-dyke. The most productive arable land was divided into strips and each tenant had a share of the good fertile pieces. Outside the head-dyke the land was held in common and each tenant was entitled to graze his animals there.

In May or June the cattle and domestic stock would be taken to the fresh green pastures of the hills in order to keep them away from the growing crops in the valleys; a migration, known as transhumance, which had been in existence for many generations. The womenfolk and children would take up residence in small roughly constructed shelters called shielings and the men would return to the valley to tend the crops and repair the houses of the townships for the wintertime. A large part of the activity at the shielings centred around the cattle; they were cared for and milked, with butter and cheese being made.

In early times shielings were built of turf or turf and stone; later shielings were of stone or, in some areas, where wood was plentiful, of timber. On occasions it was quite usual for two or more shieling grounds to be linked with one valley settlement one being more distant; this provided a better utilisation of grazing resources. Some shieling grounds today are unaltered since being abandoned and represent a way of life which has long since disappeared.

Glen Feshie is referred to as the "summer shielings of Dalnavert" in the early title deeds of Dalnavert, and there is evidence of the glen being used for grazing cattle in several place-names, Druim na Bo means *"ridge of the cattle"* and Lochan nam Bo, *"loch of the cattle"*. Evidence of shielings too is provided by the Gaelic place names Ruighe, Rie or Rea which mean *"outstretched base of a mountain, or shieling ground"*. The place-names of Righ na Bruach, Ruigh Aiteachan, and Ruigh Fionntaig are found in the glen and although the archaeological remains at these places indicate that they were townships or farmsteads in more recent times, they almost certainly started out as shieling grounds.

Documents in the Gordon papers provide firm evidence of shielings in Glen Feshie in 1682 and it would appear that even at this date some of the structures were considered as "old". Some bothies were described as "huts" indicating that they were perhaps built of wood or stone:

> Ruthven 15th Nov 1682 - the said James McPherson being further interogat anent the present seats of sheallings in the said forrest of Glenfeshie declares and names Riefuit *(Ruigh Fionntaig)* Riewaird *(Inver Eindart/Eidart)* KairnChrine *(Carnachuin)* Rieattachan *(Ruigh Aiteachan)* Rieintuim *(possibly Ruighe nan Leum)* & Straanlea *(Stronetoper)* these were of old sheallings and also Auchmacheitt *(Achleum-a-choid)* whereon he saw twelve bothies but no Cornes nor winter dwelling and being interogat where there are sheallings now that were not off old answered that there is a bothie in ...... Ailtarnagan *(Allt Fhearnagan)* and another in the foot of Corieganlach *(Coire Gharbhlach)* and frichcory *(Fionnar Choire)* and a bothie in the thrie Coireattachanes *(thought to be Coire Chaoil)* And that Tom fade were *(was)* a winter dwelling before the few *(feu)* and that there were hutts and not earthen bothies in Coireroy *(Coire Ruadh)* & Corearnagane *(Coire Fhearnagan)* (NAS GD44/27/13/1).

This document describes remote Tomfad as a winter dwelling but another document in the same papers, with details of the boundaries of the forest of "Glenfeachie", states that in Glen Feshie itself there was no winter dwelling above Tolvah. It also states that the shielings were "laboured" indicating that there was cultivation at some of the shieling grounds in the summer:

> At Ruthven 14th No[vember] 1682 - that there was no winter dwelling above tolva on both syds of the said watter and that all the sheallings above tolva were laboured Tho not dwelt upon in winter (NAS GD44/27/13/1).

Bil tells us:

> Forest owners actively encouraged settlement and agriculture in the neighbourhood of their forests even though it carried the risk of more permanent

*Glenfeshie* (also called Highland River) c1830-1835 – Courtesy of Simon C Dickinson Ltd

Slochd Beag, Upper Glen Feshie, 2005

future expansion. As early as 1669 shiels were ordered to be erected in the Forest of Atholl to counter the encroachments of people from adjoining districts of Badenoch and Mar. At the turn of the 18th century, Killiehuntley *(adjacent and to the west of Invereshie)* was ordered to grass in a place near the boundary between the Forests of Atholl and Spey, chiefly to prevent Speyside trespassers from encroaching on the grounds of the Forest of Atholl. Forest boundary keeping was an important function of shielings. It was not unknown though for grazing pressure within the forest to rise beyond the carrying capacity of the land where overstocked shielings competed too successfully with the deer and very often shieling activities were banned or resited to less exhausted zones of the forest (Bil, 1990).

Glen Feshie would, at one time, have had significant woodland cover but over the years the impact of human habitation with the use of timber for building materials, for firewood and the effect of grazing animals was to lead to significant deforestation. This deforestation was taking place throughout the Highlands and there was increasing concern amongst landowners who wished to preserve the woodland in order to exploit it for profit themselves. In 1719 the proprietor of the Mar Estate, adjacent to Glen Feshie, reached an agreement with his tenants limiting their use of timber:

> the removal of fir timber, except for use in roof couples or of fir branches for cabers or rafters was banned, furthermore, no timber was to be used for the walls of shieling huts, fencing yards or corn-stacks (NAS GD124/17/121/1, RCAHMS, 1995).

Tenants were encouraged to build stone structures which did not use the same amount of timber, and in addition were considered to be healthier although not as warm as turf bothies. No evidence for restrictions on the use of timber in Glenfeshie was found in the documents, but a tack of 1757 given to Invereshie indicates that there was concern about the impact of settlers on the woodland:

> *(you are)* to preserve the woods growing on the said Forrest from being cutt or destroyed except for the necessary uses of the fewers & tennents of the said Duke of Gordons Lands ..... who have servitudes on the said woods for the upholding & repairing their biggings. (NAS GD44/28/15/2)

Locations which we consider today as wastelands were at one time important summer grazings for cattle. Rea Gauldy, a shieling site on the watershed between the Rivers Feshie and Geldie, was almost certainly a "boundary patrolling" shieling and Lynabirrack, also close to the watershed, was "shieled" by tenants of the neighbouring estate of Rothiemurchus. In 1712 "a tolerance" was given by the Marquis of Huntly "for favour and friendship":

> to Patrick Grant of Rothiemurchus *(I)* do hereby tolerat, permit and allow him to grass his own cattle in and about the shealing of Lynabirrack in Glenfeshie the cattoll particularly belonging to himself and now others and to continue ... during our pleasure (NAS GD44/41/63/1/3).

Reabirack *(almost certainly Lynabirrack)* is marked on the Thomson map of 1830 in the

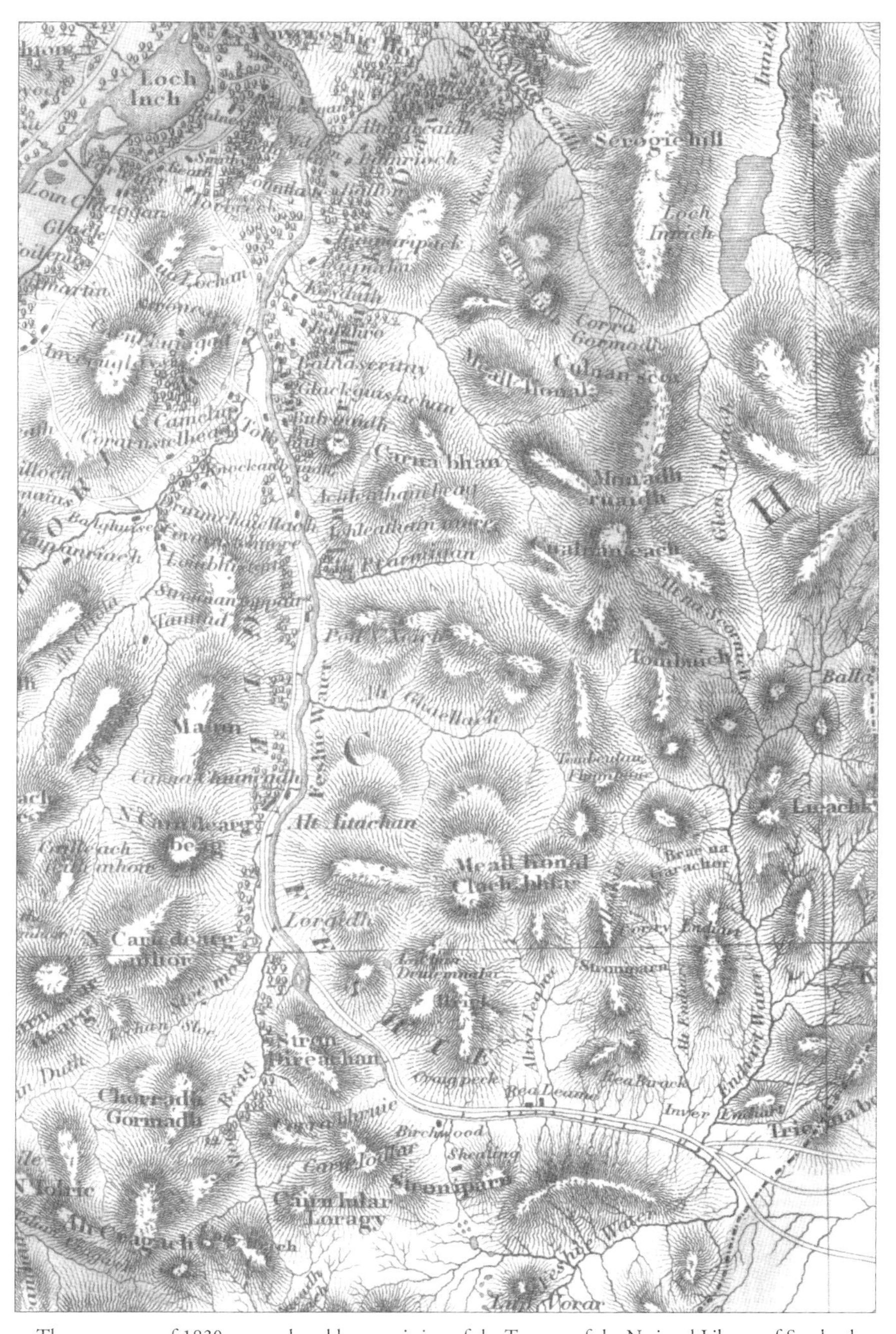


Thomson map of 1830 - reproduced by permission of the Trustees of the National Library of Scotland

lower reaches of the River Eidart. The tack for "Rienabirrack" was renewed in 1766 but in 1771 George Macpherson of Invereshie disputes it and in 1776 Rothiemurchus is warned out of "the sheallings of Glenfeshie"

George Brown, land surveyor, indicates that some of these remote shielings were still used in the 19th Century. In his report of 1803, "The State and Situation of the Forrest of Feshie" he writes:

> This forest is divided into two by the Water of Feshie *(which)* turns westwards at the shealing of Rea Gaudy *(Geldie)*....... Besides the shealings of Rie Leume and Inver Endart and indeed all along the north side of the river *(Feshie)* is very good sheep ground and well sheltered ....... when Geo Brown went over the ground, Invereshies sheep stock was all there, and upon that part to the south, first mentioned, many cattle and horses of his tenants (NAS GD44/51/732/29).

Today there is evidence of more recent adaptation and reuse of many of these higher shielings; they probably provided shelter for the shepherds and "forward bases" for the shooting parties which began to frequent the area in the 1830s

The decline of the shieling system is complex and variable and came about over a considerable period of time. The main factor, arguably, was population increase which led to pressure on land; permanent occupation of the shieling grounds was an obvious result. But equally the conversion of the shieling areas into hill grazing for sheep and later the establishment of deer forests played its part. The potato too has been suggested as a factor; it had become one of the staples in the diet of the Highlander and needed more attention in the summer months compared to the traditional bere and oats, this meant that the people were not as free to go to the hills.

The shielings of Achleum-a-choid, Righ na Bruach, Stronlia and Ruigh Fionntaig, all mentioned in the 1682 list, became permanent settlements in the 18th century but it is difficult to establish the precise date of this colonisation. It seems to have been before 1750 when the townships are marked on the Roy map with cultivation strips surrounding them. In Coire Fhearnasdail too strips surround the townships of Knockinbui, Lynavragit and Corarnstilmor and even remote Tomfadh has its fair share. The 1682 document has Auchmacheitt *(Achleum-a-choid)* described as "having no cornes", presumably meaning no summer cultivation and even by 1726 it is unclear whether there was summer cultivation. Fraser-Mackintosh tells us:

> in 1726 John Shaw, described as tackman of Kinrara, continuing in favour with his chief, obtains a tack of that part of Dalnavert called Iosal of Croftbeg and of Achleum-a-choid in Glenfeshie....... and also in 1734 gets a new lease of the 3 ploughs of Kinrara-na-Choille *(now Inshriach)* and of Rie na Bruach in Glenfeshie (Fraser Mackintosh, 1898)

The earliest firm documentary evidence for settlement in the glen was 1768; Donald Gollanach and John Kennedy were paying rent for Achlean Beag (NRAS 771/Bundle 209) and in 1770 38 wedders were delivered to Donald Macpherson at Achlean (NRAS

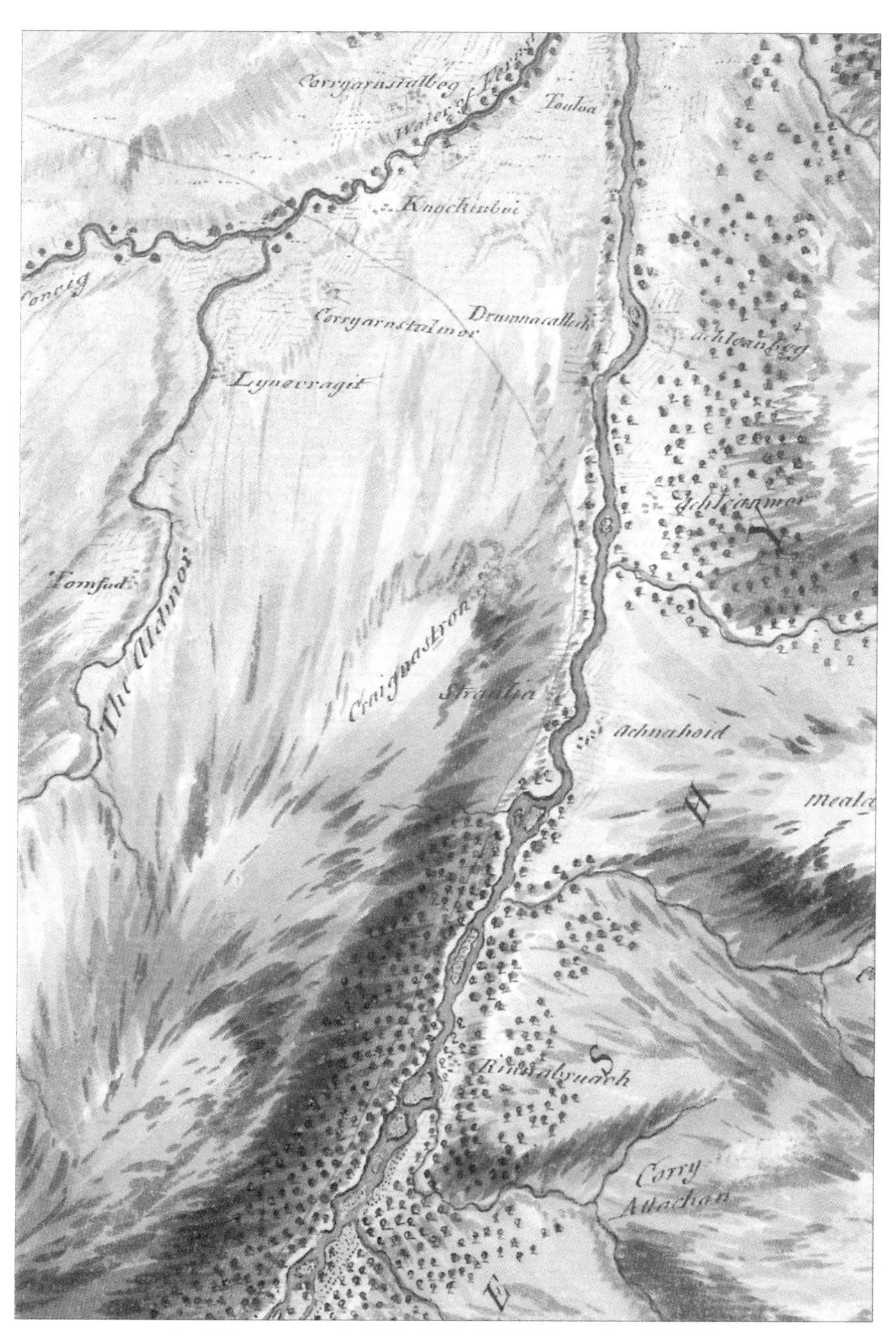


Roy Military survey of c1750 - © The British Library Board/SCRAN

Looking towards Corrie Garbhalach from the northwest. The remains of the townships of Achleum-a-choid and Strounantobhair are seen on either side of the "pony bridge", the excavated cairns are mid-left on the far side of the river

The heather covered footings of the buildings at Achleum-a-choid township

771/Bundle 209). In a list of farming equipment sold to tenants dated 1772 (NRAS 771/Bundle 129), John Shaw resided at Tolva, Evan McIntosh is at Stronetobar *(Stronlia)*; Achlemecht *(Achleum-a-choid)* has Donald Robertson and Rinabruigh has Robert Kennedy. In the upper part of the glen the first mention of Ruifuintaich *(Ruigh Fionntaig)* is 1799 when the tenant, possibly a sheepfarmer, paid rent of £85 (NRAS 771/Bundle 987) and at Carnachuin in 1805, William Mitchell received 116 wedders and 105 ewes from Donald Stewart, Invereshie's shepherd (NRAS 771/bundle 94).

Human occupation in the glen then, was limited only to the summer months for several centuries and the period of permanent colonization was to last for a relatively short time, perhaps 50 years, before the shepherds moved in.

**The Archaeology of Shielings and Townships**

In earlier times shieling huts were constructed of turf or turf and stone and their remains today have an oval grassy mounded form often with a "dished" centre. Later shielings were rectangular and of stone construction (Fenton 1976, Bil 1990). Often groups of huts might number as many as 20 or 30 at one site, or they might be in pairs, when the smaller hut would have served as a dairy. Huts of both types of construction at one site might signify long use as a shieling ground

The physical remains of shielings were found at ten, possibly twelve, locations in Glen Feshie and nearly all are mentioned in the 1682 document with at least four of the sites later developed as permanent settlements as previously mentioned. In 2004 and 2006 members of the North of Scotland Archaeological Society excavated three of the clearance cairns at Achleum-a-choid and discovered that they had buildings, which were interpreted as shielings, underlying them. The cairns were of similar shape, size and alignment and had been formed by dumping stones from the fields into a convenient uncultivateable spot, in this case, ruined buildings. One of the excavated buildings had three circular stone recesses with cobbled bases against its north wall; these were thought to have been safe places for storing wooden milk "coggies". Another building had small mounds at each corner which were revealed as part of a sophisticated blocking system for "tail forks", cabers which would have supported the end of the building. Several other cairns of similar shape size and alignment were noted at Achleum-a-choid and also at Righ na Bruach and it can be safely assumed that they too will have the remains of bothies underlying them.

At Strounantobhar (Stronlia) there are the substantial remains of three buildings with turf walls and rounded corners and at Ruigh Fionntaig the turf footings of 5 buildings with rounded corners; both of these sites are mentioned in the 1682 document. The structures may have been shielings which have undergone a different history to those on the east side of the river. At the current Ruigh Aiteachan no evidence of shielings was found, it may be that subsequent activity has completely destroyed them or it is possible that the name has been transferred from the site of the present Righ na Bruach. The name Righ na Bruach does not appear in the 1682 shieling list but "Rieattachan" does. The present Righ na Bruach on the fluvial outwash of the Allt Coire Chaoil is an obvious place for settlement and the Allt Coire Chaoil was formerly named the Allt Aitachan on the Thomson map of 1830, in addition the Roy map of c1750 has Corry Attachan marked in the upper reaches of the burn. Higher up the glen the shieling site of Ruigh Chreagan has 10 bothies some of turf and some of stone, suggesting a long period of occupancy. In the hills to the west of Glenfeshie Lodge three extensive early shieling sites are to be found; one, on the banks of the Allt Coire nam Mart *("burn of the corrie of the cow")*, NN 8186 9411, has 22 turf and stone bothies and the other two, at Feith Mor, NN 8059 9235 and NN 8050 9218, have 20 and 13 turf shielings respectively.

With an abundance of trees in the glen some shieling bothies would have been built of timber; the location of these is now difficult to detect as the timbers will have rotted away. But occasionally the location of one of these buildings may be indicated by an obvious manmade grassy platform and just such a platform is seen in Coire Fhearnagan. It may have been a shieling but equally it may have been a timber building constructed for the shooting parties in the 19th century. Later stone built shielings were found at four sites in the upper glen - Ruighe nan Leum, Inver Eindart, Rea Gauldy, and Sron na Ban-righ. At each of the sites there was between three and seven buildings and many

Member of NOSAS at work excavating the cairns at Achleum-a-choid

The cairn at Achleum-a-choid with the mounds at each corner barely discernible

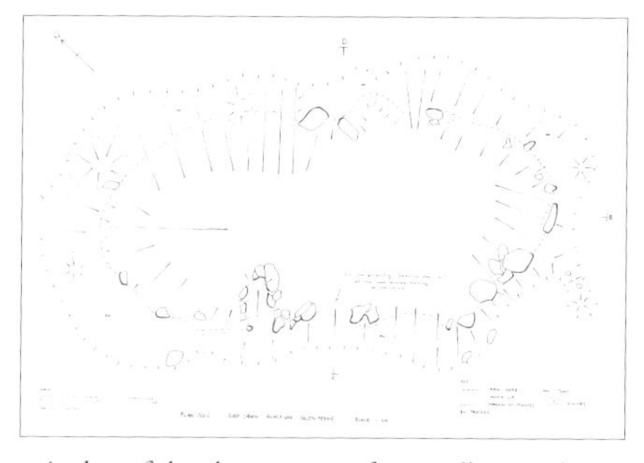

A plan of the above cairn – five small mounds are seen, one at each corner and one part way along the side where the entrance to the structure would have been located.

A reconstruction of a building in the Highland Folk Museum, Newtonmore, showing "tail-forks" supporting the gable end.

Wooden "coggies" were used for storing milk

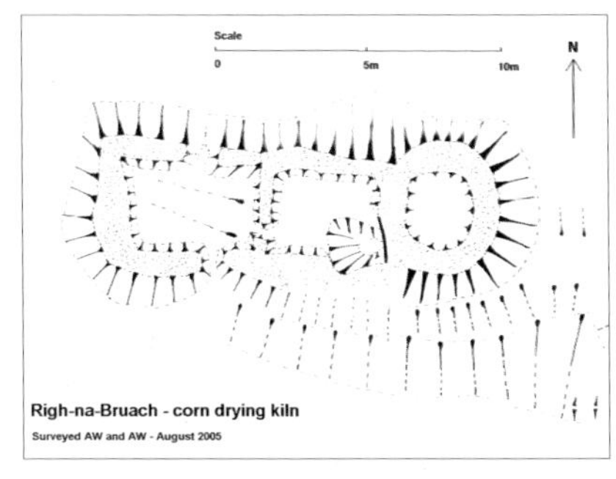


The corn drying kiln at Righ na Bruach with a plan above. The bowl is seen to the rear and the flue entrance in the foreground. The hearth would have been in front of the flue; warm air was drawn up through the grain which was placed on a mesh in the kiln.

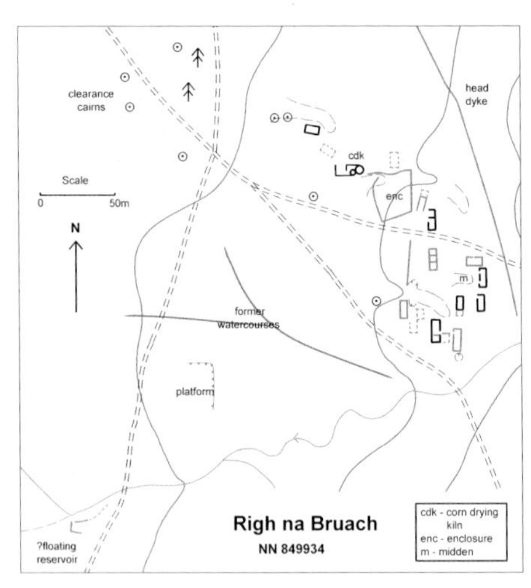


2005 survey of the township of Righ na Bruach showing typical components of a township – buildings, enclosure, corn drying kiln, head dyke, midden and clearance cairns.

had been altered and re-used more recently, probably by the shepherds or the sporting fraternity. Sron na Ban-Righ *("the nose of the white queen")* is in an elevated position and reached by an old stalkers path, with the ruins of a bridge over the river at the foot of the slope.

Defining the characteristics of a township is not always straight-forward. The basic format is a cluster of buildings accompanied by an area of cultivated, often rigged ground. There can be many variations on this - enclosures of varying dimensions, corn-drying or lime kilns, byres, middens, storage pits, stack stands and headwalls. The buildings of early townships were of turf or turf and stone and had rounded corners, today their remains appear as low footings but they are often difficult to detect because they have been replaced by larger stone-built houses with squared corners.

Seven townships are seen in Glen Feshie today and all have the remains of buildings which are generally substantial and built of stone. All the sites are marked on the Roy map of c1750; Achlean Beg, Achlean Mhor, Achleum-a-choid and Righ na Bruach on the east bank of the river and Tolva, Druimcaillich, and Strounanthobair/Stronlia on the west. The township at Achleum-a-choid, which lies 800m south of the keepers cottage presently known as Achleum, is typical of the townships in the glen. It has the stone footings of 6 buildings, a corn-drying kiln, an enclosure and extensive cultivation remains. The corn drying kiln was an essential feature of every township as the climate in the Highlands could not be relied upon to dry the corn effectively. Many of the corn drying kilns in Glen Feshie are clearly identifiable, the one at Righ na Bruach being a particularly good example.

**Cattle Rieving**

An Sgarsoch, on the Atholl boundary to the south of the glen, is reputed in local folklore to have been the location of a horse and cattle market. It is a remote spot near the junction of the three counties of Perth, Aberdeen and Inverness and may have been a convenient place for dealing in goods, many of which were contraband (Mitchell, 1999, Haldane, 1997). The rieving or thieving of cattle was an age old tradition in the Scottish Highlands. In some respects it was as much a sport where clan warriors, keen to show their skill and judgment, descended from the hills to carry off their neighbour's stock.

Documents provide evidence, albeit in the later years of the 17th and 18th centuries, of cattle rievers passing through Glen Feshie. But the clansmen who returned to the ways of cattle raiding at this time did so in order to survive and were in fact Jacobites, fighting a doomed guerilla campaign and struggling against a government army that had a garrison in practically every glen. Jacobite rievers from Lochaber and Badenoch, destitute following the "scorched earth" policy of the government after the Battle of Culloden, travelled the route through Glen Feshie and Glen Geldie, making regular raids and bringing cattle back from the fertile lands of Aberdeen and the east. The folk in the Glen Feshie area were not innocent of the activity either! An agreement (NAS

GD52/80) was drawn up in 1696 between William, Lord Forbes, and John Shaw of Dalnavert for the discovery and prosecution of those responsible for a Highland raid on the townlands of Edinbanchory *(in lower Deeside)* in October 1689. Whether the culprits were found or not will probably never be known! But there were attempts by the local lairds to control the raids. In 1744, Evan Macpherson of Cluny:

> regularly stationed his men on such passes and inlets through which the thievish sett used to make their incursions giving them strict orders that these passes should be punctually travelled and watched night and day (Spalding Club Miscellany, 1843 - *"a brief account of the rise and progress of the watch undertaken by Evan Macpherson of Cluny in 1744 for the security of severall countrys in the North of Scotland from Thrifts and Depradations").*

Cattle raiding may have been the reason for the Duke of Gordon giving Macpherson of Invereshie a warrand in 1727:

> You are to allow no Horse or other Cattle to be within the forrest of Glenfeshie or any persone to travell through the same with gunns - upon any pretext whatsoever and in caice you find any horse or other cattle in the said fforrest you are to take them and pursue the owners and dispose of the cattle conform to law as also those who carry guns (NAS GD 44/28/15/1).

Haldane informs us:

> After 1746 the authorities set their minds to the task of bringing peace and security to the Highlands. The protection of this area *(Moray, Aberdeen and the east)* from cattle raiding was one of their main preoccupations. The key to the problem lay in the guarding of a line running from Blair Atholl through the Pass of Drumochter to the Upper Spey and the securing of the glens east of that line. Memoranda of 1744 and 1747 detail the measures proposed to check cattle thieving. Small military detachments were to be posted at various points on a line between Blair Atholl in the south and Ruthven in the north, with key points to control such passes. These points included ... Dalnacardoch and Dalwhinnie, Glenfeshie and Glenclunie ..... and the establishment of a garrison in Glen Feshie in 1747 shows it to have been recognized at that date as a raider's route (Haldane, 1997).

On the watershed between the Rivers Feshie and Geldie, at grid reference NN 914873, there are the substantial stone footings of two rectangular buildings. It is a wild and hostile place at an altitude of 500m with extensive views down both glens and is probably one of the garrisons. The site is marked on Roys military map of c1750 as "Slionavaity"

**Cattle Droving**

Following the Union of the Crowns of Scotland and England in 1603, and particularly after the Act of Union of Scotland and England in 1707, a bigger market became available for the produce of Scotland. The demand for beef from the large centres of population was such that the export of cattle became a large part of the Scottish economy. By the middle of the 17th century the droving trade had grown to a huge operation and many opportunities had arisen for drovers. In 1663, 18,574 cattle were recorded as passing through Carlisle on the border between Scotland and England. In the latter half of the 18th century a series of overseas conflicts led to yet more demand for beef, this time for salt beef from the Navy. By the end of the century total exports of cattle from Scotland had quintupled with cattle prices rising fourfold (Devine, 1994). For over two hundred years, from the early seventeenth century to the early nineteenth century, droving flourished and was assisted by a growing human population in the great industrial cities of the south.

The skills required for cattle rustling were also those for droving. The rievers of one century were to become the legitimate drovers of the next. As population numbers grew in the Highlands in the second half of the 18th century more revenue was needed to feed more mouths; rearing and exporting cattle became crucial. The Highlanders would sell their cattle to the drovers who would move them on to the trysts of Falkirk or Crieff and sell them to others who, in turn, would take them to the grazing areas of Northumberland or the Yorkshire Dales in northern England where they would be fattened up before the final journey to London and the south.

Glen Feshie was a droving route, although not the main one, for cattle passing from the north to the markets in the south. The tenants of the glen would have made their small contribution to the drove. The Old Statistical Account (1792) for the parish of Alvie tells us that the tenants paid their rents in cash from the increase in sale of cattle. In 1806 the grazing in the glen is advertised to let:

> This forest *(of Glenfeshie)* contains about 1300 acres and affords excellent pasture for sheep, black cattle and hill horses. It is situated directly on the road from Inverness to the South Country markets and the confines of Aberdeen and Perthshire, it must be an object well worth attention of dealers in cattle in all corners of the kingdom – graziers from England and the South of Scotland might find their account in making a depot for cattle brought from the north during the summer and the autumn (NAS GD44/28/15/5).

George Macpherson of Invereshies' offer (NAS GD/44/28/15/7) to rent the ground was accepted and he was to lease the lands from the Duke of Gordon in 1812.

The cessation of the Napoleonic Wars and the peace after the battle of Waterloo in 1815 led to more competition from abroad and the demand for beef from the Highlands declined. With the price of cattle dipping and the discharge of many soldiers home to the Highlands more pressure fell on the Highland economy. Export of cattle continued on a much smaller scale for a further century and there is evidence that Glen Feshie was still in use as a droving route in the middle of the 19th century:

> Litigation (Scottish Rights of Way v. Macpherson, Court of Session Cases 1887)..... the evidence of drovers who appeared before the Court suggests that

> the *(droving)* route through Glen Feshie and Glen Geldie was in regular use till the middle of the 19th century (Haldane 1997).

Droving declined gradually over the 19th Century as steamships provided a faster and easier alternative to the long arduous overland journeys and, by 1880, railways too were to give an even swifter and more reliable means of transporting cattle.

But lack of demand for beef from the south was not the only factor which led to the decline of cattle rearing and droving. In the late 18th century the land that had supported a population with their black cattle began to be turned over to sheep as a process known as "Improvement" swept through the Highlands. Landowners looked for ways to make their land give them a better return and saw large scale sheep farming as the answer. "Improvement" meant that the old run-rig form of cultivation, with several tenants occupying a piece of land, was replaced by a single sheep farming unit (Fenton, 1976). For a time sheep farming and the old way of life co-existed in Glen Feshie. George Brown noted in his survey of 1803

> when Geo Brown went over the ground Invereshie's sheep stock was all there, and upon that part to the south, first mentioned, many cattle and horses of his tenants (NAS GD44/51/732/29)

In 1808 cattle still played a significant part in the revenue of some of the tenants on the Invereshie estate. In a letter to Invereshie, Alexander Bell in Coranstilbeg reports that Donald Fraser bought 24 cows without calves from him (NRAS 771/Bundle 1230). Many tenants however were unable or reluctant to take on the new ways of "Improvement", the odds were against them and many were to drift away in the next few decades.

## 3. The "Improvement" Period and Sheep Farming.

The late 18th century was a time of great change in the Highlands. Landowners began to introduce sheep to their estates on a large scale as the culture of "Improvement" swept through the country. This radical change was brought about by the influences of the more prosperous country to the south. From early times Highland gentry had been in contact with their counterparts in the South; it had been traditional for the sons of Highland chiefs to be raised in the households of families in other parts of Scotland or in England and to attend University or to travel in Europe. Following the Act of Union of Scotland and England in 1707, the landed gentry of Scotland were subjected to the ways of the aristocracy in the south to an even greater extent. They tried to match and even compete with a society which was becoming increasingly wealthy through industrialisation. The process of "Improvement" was a completely new way forward for farming. In addition to sheep-rearing, it involved the enclosure of land and the improvement of soil by adding lime and rotating the crops, the reclamation of waste land by ditching and draining, the introduction of new and improved breeds of cattle and sheep and better housing for everyone. These new measures started slowly but following the rebellion of 1746 they gathered momentum and were to have a profound effect on the population of the Highlands.

Sheep had been reared alongside cattle, horses and goats on Badenoch lands for many years; in 1637 a charter granted to Angus Macpherson of Invereshie by George, Marquis of Huntly, stated that the payment:

> for the towns and lands of Invereshie, Cultaloid and Coirarnsdalemore *(would be)* the sume of Fifty marks Scots money.... together with two wedders in lamb, two goose, ane stone of butter and ane ? of poultry (NAS GD 44/28/7/1/1)

It is not clear when the new breed of sheep were introduced to Glen Feshie. Meta Scarlett tells us that it was c1750, but does not quote the sources of her information:

> About 1750 Gaick and Glenfeshie forests were let as runs for sheep imported from the Borders (Scarlett, 1988).

By 1770 it seems that a good number of sheep were being reared on Invereshie lands; memo and cash books for the Invereshie Estate of May 1770 state that:

> eight score and eleven sheep and ? rams *(were)* delivered to John Gollanach (NRAS 771/Bundle 209)

And on 9th Feb 1786 a note tells us that Invereshie has:

> 263 sheep, 9 rams, 120 lambs and 120 wedders that the tenants have a keeping of (NRAS 771/Bundle 129)

By 1792 the Old Statistical Account (OSA) for Alvie remarks of Glenfeshie:

> The natives are remarkable for the quantity and quality of white plaiding they bring to market, all manufacturing what wool their own exigencies will permit in that manner. Their blankets and clothing have very few dyes and are extremely coarse, their plaiding sells at about 10d the ell *(39 inches)*.....
> *(In the parish)* there are 1104 black cattle, 510 horses and 7000 sheep ......There

is only one farm stocked wholly with sheep..........The country sheep are of the whitefaced kind, by introduction of the black-faced tups the breed is greatly meliorated of late but the wool is much coarser.

In the later part of the 18th century the conversion of the Highlands to sheep farming was encouraged by fairly steady growth in the demand for wool and during the Napoleonic War years of 1790 to 1815 there was a further increase when the price of wool multiplied. Tom Devine writes:

> Overseas supply of woollen manufactures from Europe was limited and erratic during the Napoleonic Wars ....... the gap was increasingly filled by Highland sheep farmers (Devine, 1994)

Sheep farmers were to compete for land in the Highlands at high rents and there was a trend towards longer leases.

In 1803 the Duke of Gordon, perhaps considering a sale of land, commissioned a survey of the upper part of Glen Feshie from George Brown. "The State and Situation of the Forrest of Feshie" is a survey of 13,706 Scots acres of land east of Craig Peek *("Craig Peck" is marked on Thomson's map of 1830 in the location of Creag Beag, GR NN 870892).* The survey gives a rosy account of the land and an indication of the attitude towards "Improvement". It makes comment that the land to the north and east of the River Feshie:

> with a south and southwest exposure, containing sundry well sheltered valuable corries, is very good sheep ground and well sheltered, and from the 10th of June till the end of September this ground alone would keep an immense number of sheep (GD 44/51/732/29)

The assessment of the survey concludes that:

> providing there was land in the Strath suitable for wintering the stock, this ground would yield £300 *(a year).* It might therefore turn out *(better)* to advertise it for sale. Some Englishman of fortune who was a sportsman might form great ideas of 13,706 Scots acres of property and there is no saying what it might bring ..... I shall only further observe, either kept as a Forrest or otherwise, his tenants would be ruined, and he obliged to curtail his sheep stock to very narrow limits. In any way of disposing of this ground, it might be proper to advertise it.

The problem, as far as sheep were concerned, was lack of ground for over-wintering them. In 1812 an advertisement appeared in the "Inverness Courier":

> ....for the forest of Glenfeshie consisting of 13,706 acres. It is adapted either for a summer grazing to black cattle or for shooting ground to a sportsman who might wish to preserve the tract for deer, moor game and ptarmigan, all of which abound in the adjoining hills and with which it would be abundantly stocked in a very short time.

George Macpherson Grant, who had inherited the Invereshie estates on the death of his uncle William Macpherson in 1812, was to purchase the Forest from the Duke of Gordon in 1816 for £3105.

*Reapers Resting, Glen Feshie,* 1827 – untraced. The skyline is that of Slochd Beag at Ruigh Fionntaig.

*Highland Breakfast, the interior of a Highland bothie,* 1834 – V&A Images/Victoria and Albert Museum

Throughout the Highlands many of the old townships with their run rig system of cultivation were combined to make way for the sheep farms. The change to sheep was to have a profound effect on the ordinary Highlander; fewer people were needed to maintain a flock of sheep and the original tenants faced difficult times. Some of the old tenants were given marginal ground at a low rent which they were expected to improve, but many were to drift away in the next few decades. In Badenoch, as in much of the Highlands, many were living in poverty, reluctant to follow the system of Improvement. The OSA of 1792 for Alvie tells us:

> The inferior tenants cannot be prevailed upon to adopt this mode of farming *(liming of land)* though very sensible of its benefits, alleging as a cause their poverty and shortness of their leases *(which are)* from 5 to 9 years........*(they)* are very poor, owing to their small holdings, and their habitations wretched ........The greatest bar to the improvement of the country is the smallness of the holdings, the shortness of the leases and not having melioration for their houses or other improvements; at present the inferior tenants consider their meliorating their houses or lands as the sure means of having an overbidder next lease.

And the OSA for Kingussie also tells us that there was little incentive for the ordinary tenant to improve his land:

> Storms are frequent at all seasons, frosts are uncommonly intense and as they continue late into spring and begin early in autumn with heavy falls of rain during the harvest months, crops are always rendered uncertain. Grazing seems to be the only kind of farming proper for this place and for this the hills in general are very suitable particularly for sheep farming......The lands in many places are only held from year to year, grassums *(fines)* are frequently exacted, additional burdens are imposed without regarding to whether they correspond with the progress of improvement and personal services are so often demanded that the tenant in many instances is more at the disposal of his landlord than the feudal vassal was of his superior in former times..........The poverty of the inhabitants may be inferred as an unavoidable consequence. An aversion to labour, combining with local disadvantages and feudal oppression cannot fail to render a peasantry poor, dispirited and comfortless. A few individuals may be found who are easy and affluent, but whoever is at pains to examine minutely the condition of the bulk of the people, to view the mean ill constructed huts in which they reside, and to consider the scanty precarious crops on which they depend will be far from thinking that the picture of their misery is drawn in exaggerated colours.

No documentary evidence for removal of people from Glen Feshie was found but there was certainly voluntary migration in the 1830s. In 1835 the New Statistical Account (NSA) for the parish of Kingussie reports that:

> The increase in population.....is greatly owing to the erection of villages which have attracted people from neighbouring parishes and would probably have been much greater were it not for emigration. No fewer than 80 souls left the united parish in 1833 for America.

In 1828 George Macpherson Grant had established the village of Insh for some of those who were displaced from Glen Feshie and Coire Fhearnasdail and in 1831 a group of six emigrants sailed from Greenock to Montreal in Canada. They included three young men from Coire Fhearnasdail; Donald MacLean from Baileguish, Peter Grant from Corarnstilmore and John Kennedy from Knockanbuie. They were to be followed by their families in 1833 and others from Tomfad and Lynavragit in 1835 and 1841. A total of 189 people from Badenoch, of whom 80 were from Glen Feshie and Coire Fhearnasdail, were to form the Badenoch settlement in Ontario. Descendents of the original emigrants of 1831 are still living there today.

It is quite probable that, with all the changes and restrictions, the people found the conditions under which they had to live quite intolerable and, "seeing the writing on the wall", decided to quit. This "push" factor would have been strong when combined with the "pull" factor of the cheap land available in Canada and reports from others who had emigrated and done very well. It seems no coincidence that 1830 was the year in which Glen Feshie was converted to a deer forest and it is possible that these people, deprived of summer grazing for their stock, found that their permanent townships were unviable. However a large population did continue in Coire Fhearnasdail; in the six settlements of Knockinbui, Corarnstilmore, Lynavragit, Tomfhad, Baileguish and Luibean Ruadh, the census of 1841 records that there was a population of 24 adults and 19 children in 10 households.

Sheep farming in Glen Feshie itself does not appear to have been very successful; hardly surprising considering the altitude, the unpredictable climate and the limited number of months when grazing was available. Giving evidence to the Napier Commission in 1884, Sir George Macpherson Grant says:

> The present proprietor is informed that forty five or fifty years ago, the then proprietor and agricultural tenants of the low grounds grazed a certain number of sheep in Glenfeshie, but the difficulty of procuring winter grazing at the early period necessary rendered the summer grazing of little value.

By 1835 many agricultural improvements had been carried out in the district. The NSA for the parish of Kingussie reports that:

> Of late years much has been done in reclaiming waste land, embanking and draining ........within the last 40 years the parish has undergone many important alterations in its physical as well as its moral character. A great part of the bleak and barren land formerly supposed fit to be only the abode of wild beasts has been brought under cultivation.......The greater part of the parish now consists of large sheepwalks.

But the minister for the parish of Alvie is critical of both landowners and tenantry. In his NSA he writes:

> The breed of sheep commonly reared is the black faced. In general no great attention has been paid to the improvement of sheep or black cattle and still less attention has been paid by the common or small tenants to the cultivation of

soil.....The absurd and unproductive system of farming pursued by their rude ancestors from time immemorial is still continued by the tenants to the deterioration of the small pendicles of land which they occupy. Another insurmountable obstacle in the way to agricultural improvement is the absurd division of land among the small tenants. It is not uncommon to see a piece of land not half an acre in extent divided into six lots called "run-rigs", which make it impossible for any one of the six to improve his small lot unless the other five concur with him...... With the exception of 2 or 3 farms there are no farm enclosures of any description in the parish and the farm buildings of the common tenants are most wretched hovels consisting of a few wooden couples joined together with cross spars and covered with a turf roof that requires to be renewed almost every second year.

All the advantages resulting from improvements are more than counterbalanced by a variety of adverse circumstances with which the farmer has to contend. Since the commencement of the late expensive war *(the Napoleonic War, 1795-1815)* besides taxes and public burdens, the rent of the land and the wages of the farm servants have been more than tripled. During the continuance of the war the price of cattle and sheep on which all Highland tenants chiefly depend was so high that the tenants were enabled to bear those heavy burdens but in the present state of things, it is entirely out of their power to pay the rents then imposed on them. Since the peace, the price of cattle has been so much reduced while the rent, the expense of farm labour and public burdens continue still the same. The unavoidable consequence of keeping up the rent in those circumstances is the accumulation of arrears to a most enormous amount.

In 1846 the population of the Highlands suffered a further blow when the potato crop was affected by "blight". This failure produced near starvation for many and a fresh wave of destitution, however the relief effort from the government and from charitable organisations was largely successful and prevented the devastating results of a similar crisis in Ireland when many had died the year before. Robert Somers visited Badenoch in 1846 and concurs with the NSA but has some different comments to make about the landed gentry:

Most of the farm houses are substantial stone fabrics, few of the black heather bothies are seen and the villages are modern and cleanly in aspect. But a close inspection convinces the inquirer that a deep stratum of wretchedness lies under the fair exterior and numerous families in poor and distressed circumstances are found living in houses which have evidently been erected when the prosperity of the district was greater and the people in much higher spirits than they are now. About 50 years ago the Duke and Duchess of Gordon were the leading magnates of the district and for a time the population shared the benefits of the princely expenditure of that family. The Duchess who was a woman of extraordinary spirit and capacity employed herself in organising and recruiting her husband's regiment of Highlanders.....In Badenoch a great proportion of the large farms are occupied by gentlemen who were at one time connected with the army. We may

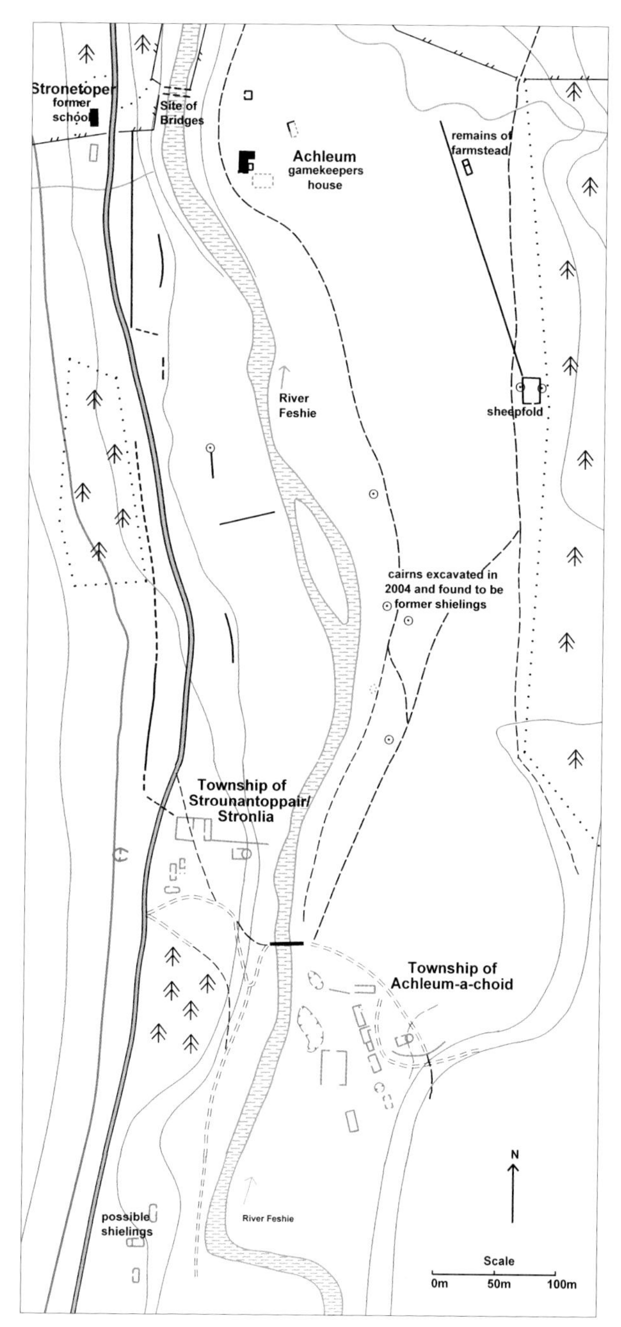


Archaeological remains at Achleum-a-choid, Strounantoppair/Stronlia and surrounding area

> be sure that however expert they might be in disposing a body of men on the battle-field, they would find that to place a few hundred scores of sheep upon a market-field to good purpose is quite a different operation. Many of them have long since become bankrupt. To make room for these gentlemen of the army the small farmers were pushed to the wall. While the village of Kingussie was in a growing state it offered asylum to the people thus cleared from the land (Somers, 1848).

These were difficult times for both tenants and landlords alike. Following the cessation of the Napoleonic Wars in 1815 the country had been able to import more provisions, the price of cattle and sheep had fallen and there had been a reduced demand for the produce of the Highlands.

Sheep farming was of limited success in Glen Feshie but, for the landowner at least, there was an alternative in the form of the "shooting let". Catering for the sporting parties became more important than sheep farming; it provided employment and prosperity for some of the local people but misery and migration for others.

**The Archaeology of Sheep Farming**

In general the rearing of sheep and sheep farming in Glen Feshie itself has had limited impact and very few archaeological remains are found. For a while at least, sheep farming and the townships seem to have survived alongside each other. At Stronetoper and Achleum there is an extensive area that could be a "sheep-park". A farmstead, sheepfold and substantial turf and stone field boundary enclosing an area approximately 600m in length on both sides of the river are seen a short distance to the north of Achleum-a-choid township. They are most likely the remnants of an early period of sheep farming, which co-existed with the cultivation and occupation of the settlement of Achleum-a-choid. At Creag na Chaillich in the upper glen a square sheepfold, with a possible sheepdip abutting, is at a particularly narrow part of the glen and in an ideal position to collect the sheep descending from the upper glen. Ruigh Fionntaig, close by and on the opposite side of the river, has the footings of a farmstead of two buildings and an enclosure at NN 847915; the Ballindalloch papers (NRAS 771/Bundle 987) has a rent of £85 being paid in 1799 for Ruifuintaich, a substantial amount possibly indicating that this was a sheep farm. From about 1825 this area was let to shooting parties and in 1830 it was converted to a "deer forest". Lower down the glen Coire Fhearnasdail continued to support a succession of farmers with sheep almost certainly bringing in a large part of their income. As previously noted the 1841 census has six settlements with a population of 24 adults and 19 children, by 1881 the population had dropped to 2 households, Corarnstilmore and Baileguish, with a population of 7 adults and 2 children. Today sheep still graze the grassy slopes in the summertime, but there is no one in permanent residence. Coire Fhearnasdail has far more evidence of sheep farming, with the remains of several sheep farms and stone built sheepfolds, both rectangular and circular. A splendid example of a circular dry-stone sheepfold is seen in the forest 1.5kms northwest of Strontoper, at grid reference NN 83687 97613.

## 4. Timber exploitation

In general it is thought that most of the destruction of woodland in the Highlands came about in the period before 1600 (Smout, 2003). In the shieling period the use of timber for buildings and for firewood and the effect of grazing animals will have undoubtedly contributed to the destruction of the woodland. But it is possible that the remoteness of Glen Feshie and its maintenance as a hunting forest in medieval times may have helped to limit the demise of its trees.

In the 18th century landowners were eager to limit the loss of woodland so that they could exploit the timber for profit themselves. On the Mar estate, adjacent to Glen Feshie, an agreement was reached in 1719 between the tenants and the landowner restricting the tenant's use of the forest and in 1726 Glen Lui was cleared of its people so that the landowner might proceed with felling and the sale of timber (RCAHMS, 1995). The Duke of Gordon too seems to have been concerned about the impact of people on his woodland; he issued a Warrand to Macpherson of Invereshie in 1727 for overseeing the forest of Glenfeshie:

> You are to allow none to cutt or destroy any of our woods within the said fforrest and to pursue those who cutt or destroy the same (NAS GD44/28/15/1)

An Avery map of 1735 marks "Firr woods" in the middle part of the glen and a saw mill on the east bank of the river, but there is no documentary evidence for the sale of timber from Glen Feshie. Perhaps the remoteness of the glen and the difficulty of transporting the timber precluded the larger scale felling that was taking place on the Mar Estate and in neighbouring Rothiemurchus and Abernethy.

The sale of timber from Glen Feshie however seems to have picked up in about 1787 and it is perhaps no coincidence that it was at a time when the felling of Rothiemurchus timber was restricted. During the 18th century attempts to exploit the Rothiemurchus timber had met with limited success and a point had been reached whereby the laird, Patrick Grant, had halted the cutting of timber for a generation in order to allow the trees to regenerate. The small size of the trees was particularly noted as one of the reasons and was attributed to the continuous exploitation of larger trees by outside entrepreneurs and the constant cutting of wood of moderate size by local folk - from 1769 to 1771 14,000 pieces of sparwood, relatively small trees, were sold as logs by local people (Smout, 1999). Another problem was the competition, both in price and quality, from Norway, but from 1780 to 1820 Norway and the Baltic were cut off from Great Britain because of the Napoleonic Wars and the market for Highland timber increased. In 1786 a shipyard had been established at Garmouth at the mouth of the River Spey, and timber for building ships was needed. The restrictions at Rothiemurchus had come at a time when the political and economic climate was exceptionally suitable for the sale of timber. It is more than probable that attention turned to neighbouring Glen Feshie. Glen Feshie was more remote but the added cost of floating the timbers the greater distance must have been felt worthwhile.

In 1785 plans were made to repair the old sawmill at Dalnavert. A letter to the Mackintosh requests:

> It being reported to us *(Margaret & Anne Shaw)* that the Miln at Dalnavert, part of your Estate under lease to us, has been neglected, and allowed to become total ruin. It is proper and necessary, for all concerned, that this Miln be repaired & rendered fit to execute the work of a Miln. *(Be)* so good as *(to)* allow the timber necessary for the repairs, to be cutt and carried off from your woods to the Miln (NAS GD176/22/19).

The earliest record for sale of timber from Glen Feshie is 1787 (NAS GD176/1582). Many others were to follow over the next 40 year period, with the latest being 1830. The "Glenfeshie Wood Company" was established sometime before 1792, when Captain Cameron and Captain John Carmichael of Kinrara, of "the Company", are reported as making a cash payment to "the Mackintosh" for wood and land rent (NAS GD176/1582). The "Glenfeshie Wood Company" is most probably the Company referred to in the Old Statistical Account below.

The passage of the timber down the Rivers Feshie and Spey was facilitated by artificial spates induced by releasing a head of water from "floating" dams in the upper glen. However all was not well with this arrangement as there were constant problems and complaints about the damage done by the spates to the embankments around the agricultural land in the lower glen. These embankments had been erected around the low lying ground adjacent to the River Spey as part of the Improvements. The OSA for Alvie in 1792 reports:

> There are a few farms having extensive meadows along the Spey which are extremely productive of grass but liable to frequent overflows to remedy which one of the most extensive meadows has been lately surrounded with an earthen bank by the proprietor

Unfortunately the induced spates breached these banks and resulted in flooding around Invereshie and Dalnavert. In 1797 the Shaws of Dalnavert were charged with contravention of their tack for allowing damage to their lands (NAS GD176/882). Bulwarks were constructed to protect the lands but this action led to flooding of neighbouring lands. There is evidence in the documents of much disagreement and bad feeling between the landowners and references were found for the repair of bulwarks in 1798, 1804, 1810 and 1814.

Although timber from Glen Feshie was being sold on a larger scale, the OSA for Alvie Parish records in 1792 that, as in Rothiemurchus, the local people were also exploiting the woodland:

> The parish abounds with fir, birch, alder and a few oaks, one proprietor only has exclusive right to the woods on his own estate who is lately let a lot of it to a Company which will probably bring him £2000. The other woods are subjected to a servitude (ie all the feuars have an equal privilege) which is a great loss to the proprietors and on the whole a disadvantage to the tenants as on this account no

> melioration is allowed for houses and now all the principal wood is mangled and destroyed by this libertine mode of cutting, so that they can hardly be supplied from them with the necessary timber. The inferior tenants .... procure their little necessities from the market towns by the sale of small parcels of wood they bring thither (distant 40 miles).

The peace following the Napoleonic Wars in 1815 meant that restrictions on imports could be lifted, but the demand for timber from the Highlands continued because import duties had been placed on foreign wood in an attempt to stimulate the Canadian timber trade. Felling in Strathspey continued until 1830-31 when competition from America and Norway led to its gradual demise.

The timber from Glen Feshie was floated a distance of 45 kilometres down the rivers to the shipbuilding yard at Garmouth. Two possible sites in upper Glen Feshie have been identified as "floating" reservoirs from which the water would have been released to assist the operation. One is at Righ na Bruach, NN 8463 9369, where there is a three sided enclosure with turf walls 1m in height; a low bank forms a channel which would have ducted water into the reservoir from a nearby stream. The second site is on the west side of the River Feshie, south of Glenfeshie Lodge; a small pond, now grossly silted up, at NN 842927, has the remains of an artificial retaining bank. Both of these sites are well positioned for their task.

Ruigh Aiteachan, 2005

*Scottish Landscape: Bringing in the Stag,* 1830, by Fredrick Richard Lee and Sir Edwin Landseer - © Tate, London, 2011. It appears that the houses in this painting are those of the north group on the First Edition OS map.

# 5. Dalnavert and the Military Tradition

Dalnavert is mentioned in 1338 as the late residence of Farqhuar Shaw, steward to Comyn, the Lord of Badenoch. The family of Shaw have a very ancient lineage and were one of the founding families of the Clan Mackintosh. From 1236 they held lands around Rothiemurchus but these lands fell into the hands of the Grants in the 16th century. By c1620 the Shaws occupied Dalnavert and South Kinrara, holding the lands on tack from the Mackintosh of Mackintosh. Dalnavert passed down through the family or near relatives until the early 19th century when the male line died out and it then passed to Margaret, niece of Thomas Shaw, who was married to Captain Alexander Clark of Invernahavon.

Elizabeth Grant of Rothiemurchus has an account of visiting Dalnavert and of the funeral of the last Shaw, Major Thomas Shaw in 1812:

> The next death was the Shaw. He was not the lineal heir of the old race, he was descended collaterally from a former chief of the ruined clan, of whose once large possessions nothing now remains but the little farm of Dalnavert. Mr Shaw was a major in the Regiment and for so old a man a good officer. He had served in the line in his youth. When we went to the "Reviews" we always called at the house of Dalnavert, a mere black peat bothy, no better outside than the common huts of the same material. It was larger, for it contained three rooms each of which had a window of four panes, not made to open. It had two chimneys or rather, only one chimney and two chimney tops open wooden ones for the kitchen fire place was as usual, a stone on the floor and a hole in the roof. Between the parlour and the bedroom a chimney stalk was built. Both these rooms too were wainscoted, so they looked neat within and were extremely warm. It was the old house that had come down with the few fields round about it to this only survivor of his Line and he would not change it. He had one child, a daughter, married away from him to a half pay Captain in the marines. Major Shaw died and was buried with full military honours in the kirkyard of Rothiemurchus. My father had a neat stone slab on four short pillars placed over it afterwards with a short inscription and so ended this ancient feud. I never could see any of the Shaw's descendents in the lowly state to which they were then reduced without an uneasy feeling. Miss Jean Shaw did not long survive her brother. When she died the niece and her husband, Captain and Mrs Clark left the farm they had rented in Invernahavon and came with their large and wonderfully handsome family to Dalnavert, where they built a small stone and lime house and the old Shaw blood raised its head a bit (Grant, 1898).

Soldiering was a part of the Highland tradition; from medieval times clansmen had provided loyalty and military service to their chief in return for land and protection. At the end of the 18th century Great Britain was involved in a succession of overseas conflicts and Highland chiefs provided the British army with military battalions drawn from their clansmen to fight in these wars. The recruits were undoubtedly attracted by the promise of security of their tenancies at a reduced rate on their return from hostilities. Many Highlanders fought in the American War of Independence (1775-1783) and the Napoleonic Wars (1795-1815). In 1789 rumours of a French invasion alarmed the country and Jane, Duchess of Gordon, had a wager with the Prince Regent as to which of them could raise a regiment more quickly. Together with her son George, Lord Huntly, the Duchess was responsible for raising the Gordon Highlanders. The pair visited every country fair in the Badenoch and Strathspey district, accompanied by six pipers and a plentiful supply of silver shillings. It is said that the Duchess invited the recruit to come up and take the shilling in his lips from between her own; by this unique method she soon raised a regiment which later was to become the 92nd or Gordon Highlanders.

Elizabeth Grant writes of the year 1809:

> During the winter my father was very much occupied with drilling his Volunteers. There were several local companies and my father was the Lieutenant-Colonel. Most of the elders had served in the regular Army and had retired in middle life upon their half pay to little Highland farms.......It was the terror of Napoleon's expected invasion that roused a patriotic fever amongst our mountains where the alarm was so great that every preparation was in train for repelling the enemy. The volunteers were drilled, exercised and inspected till the year 1813. It was a very pretty sight on the beautiful meadows of Dalnavert to come suddenly on this fine body of men and the gay crowd collected to look at them (Grant, 1898).

Following the conflicts the military gentlemen returned home to the farms which had been "reserved" for them. Dalnavert seems to have had a good quota of retired military officers. Major Thomas Shaw, already mentioned, was the tacksman until his death in 1812. He was succeeded by his niece and her husband, Captain Alexander Clark who in turn were followed by their son Captain James Clark. Captain James Cameron and Captain John Carmichael, in South Kinrara *(Inshriach)* from 1789, have already been mentioned as establishing the Glenfeshie Wood Company.

Robert Somers is very scathing of the "military" landlords. He writes:

> In Badenoch a great proportion of the large farms are occupied by gentlemen who were at one time connected with the army. A stranger is amazed at the majors, the captains and lieutenants with whom he finds a peaceable country so thickly planted and they are all Macphersons or Mackintoshes. These gentlemen are officers who have received their respective commissions from the Duchess of Gordon and who on returning home from the wars founded upon their services in the field a claim to a comfortable agricultural settlement. Their demand was allowed, but these military farmers, generally speaking, have not been successful. ..... we may be sure that however expert they might be in disposing a body of men on the battle-field, they would find that to place a few hundred scores of sheep upon a market-field to good purpose is quite a different operation. Many of them have long since become bankrupt (Somers, 1848).

Whether or not this is true of the tacksmen at Dalnavert is difficult to determine. Certainly the OSA of 1792 for Alvie is complementary of Major Thomas Shaw's management of his property:

> .... the most extensive meadows *(at Dalnavert)* has been lately surrounded with an earth bank by the proprietor which rescues it completely from the summer and harvest floods so that rich crops of corn can be now safely raised where the grass was formerly precarious.

And in 1835 the NSA for Alvie parish:

> Considerable improvements in agriculture have been made of late by a few individuals. At Dalnavert, also the property of the Laird of Mackintosh, Mr James Clark the present tacksman nearly doubled the arable land of that farm by draining, grubbing and embanking since he came into possession of it....... *(However)* all the advantages resulting from improvements are more than counterbalanced by a variety of adverse circumstances with which the farmer has to contend. Since the commencement of the late expensive war *(the Napoleonic War, 1795-1815)* the rent of the land and the wages of the farm servants have been more than tripled. During the continuance of the war the price of cattle and sheep on which all Highland tenants chiefly depend was so high that the tenants were enabled to bear those heavy burdens but in the present state of things, it is entirely out of their power to pay the rents imposed on them. Since the peace, the price of cattle has been so much reduced while the rent, the expense of farm labour and public burdens continue still the same. The unavoidable consequence of keeping up the rent in those circumstances is the accumulation of arrears to a most enormous amount.

Lapses in payment of rent were a regular occurrence in the Highlands at this time, almost certainly a sign of hard times. A deduction was authorised for the tenants of Dalnavert and Kinrara in a rental of 1826-27 (NAS GD128/11/1) "in consequence of the depressed state" and in 1832-33 there are "accounts and correspondence relating to arrears of rent due by Captain James Clark for Dalnavert and Kinrara" (NAS GD176/1314).

*The Illicit Highland Whisky Still,* 1826-29 – © English Heritage

A sketch of an illicit whisky still from 1827

# 6. Illicit Pleasures - Whisky and Poaching

In the 1780s a change in the legislation governing the production of whisky led to a huge increase in illegal production of the spirit throughout the Highlands. The rise was attributed to the increase in tax on small stills and on the malt used; this led to legal whisky becoming inferior but yet more costly. A golden opportunity for smugglers in the Highlands was provided from 1790 to 1823 and the market was flooded with illicit spirit as the law was flouted on a massive scale. Highland whisky was in great demand and satisfying this demand provided an important source of revenue for the Highlander. Illicit distillation flourished for nearly 50 years and numerous stories are told of the illicit distillers and their adventures; fake funeral processions travelled long distances with the spirit concealed in the coffin and women were seen going to market with sudden advanced "pregnancies" for example. Often the whole family was involved, the womenfolk playing a big part in producing the spirit and the children keeping a look-out for "gaugers", as the excise men were known.

The measures to restrict the illegal production of whisky were, in general, ineffective and often only nominal fines were imposed by the courts. The dilemma of the justices at Dingwall was put by Sir George Mackenzie of Coul in his evidence to a government enquiry in 1822:

> When we sit in judgement and we see before us our own tenants, we know that when we inflict even the lowest penalty directed by law, if the tenant be able to pay *(the fine)* he will not pay his rent and if he is not able to pay, we must send him to prison where he can do nothing to help his affairs while in the meantime his family is starving on account of being deprived of help or attempting to find relief by conduct far worse than defrauding the revenue - if our tenants fall we must fall along with them (British Parliamentary Papers Vol VII *"Inquiry into the Revenue arising in Ireland etc"*, 1823)

Illicit distillation was even encouraged by the landowners! - it provided cash to pay an inflated rent to a landlord who would "turn a blind eye" to the practice. The excise men, given their difficult task in such circumstances, had abandoned trying to enforce the law and many had resorted to exploiting the situation by appropriating the malt duties for themselves. In 1792 the OSA for Alvie reports:

> They *(the people)* are much addicted to drinking of whisky, whence at their public meetings (such as burials &c) squabbles are frequent. Their fondness for spirits is owing to the easy access to it, there being no less than 13 houses in the parish where drams are sold without a county or excise licence, to the very great prejudice of the purse, constitution and morals of the natives. Such a nuisance to society is overlooked by the proper *(excise)* officer on account of the trouble and distance from the County town and the proprietors also residing at a distance.

The illicit industry gradually collapsed following legislation in 1823 which reduced the tax on the malt and increased the powers of the excise men. Legal whisky became more competitive in price and by 1835 the NSA for Kingussie records:

> Smuggling, which at one time prevailed to a great extent and tended more to demoralise the people, has been of late entirely abandoned and a sensible amelioration in the morals of the inhabitants has in consequence taken place.

The archaeological remains of still bothies are not impressive and generally difficult to identify. Many of the stills would have been improvised affairs with no regular form and the apparatus of pot-still and worm will have been removed. The only consistent features of the sites are that they are in secret, remote locations and close to a source of running water. Many of the sites have the remains of small buildings constructed of dry stone or turf. Generally they are recessed into a bank or against a crag, so that they could have been easily camouflaged by covering them with branches and turves. One such site was found in Coire Fhearnasdail at NN 8265 9609 *(NMRS No - NN89NW 09, HER ID - MHG 24926).* It is in a small ravine not too far from the township of Tomfad and comprises the substantial remains of a small building with roughly constructed dry stone walls c0.5m high. It is recessed into a steep heathery slope and beside a small burn. We cannot be sure that this was the site of an illicit still but it is in an ideal location. Sir Edwin Landseer painted a number of pictures of illicit stills and it is quite possible that they were scenes in the vicinity of Glen Feshie.

The act of poaching with all its elements of risk and adventure was similar to that of whisky distilling and appealed strongly to the romantic artist Landseer. He was particularly fond of painting scenes which depicted the ordinary life of the people of the Highlands; in addition to cottage interiors and illicit stills he painted several "poaching" scenes, but it is known that his subjects were in the employment of the Invereshie estate as stalkers. In the early 19th century the skills of a poacher were recognized as being ideally suited to stalking and in the early days of the sporting estates the title poacher and stalker were interchangeable. William Collie writes:

> My father was born in 1795 at Rothiemurchus. He was a great poacher, but as he generally sent the lion's share of his sport to the Doune *(of Rothiemurchus)* he was allowed to roam about more in the capacity of a keeper......There were then only five deer forests in Scotland, with probably one stalker in each (Collie, 1908).

Later William Collie describes incidents of illegal poaching in Glenfeshie:

> In 1833, Glenfeshie was made a forest by the Hon Edward Ellice MP and my father was appointed head forester. There were several wild smugglers and poachers in Glenfeshie and my father wanted an assistant. After a while a very strong handsome man, Donald Fraser, appeared. My father had troublous times with three brothers who were great smugglers and poachers and lived with their father on a different estate and could not be ejected. One of the sons probably in the hope that it might reform him was made a forester but he retained all his poaching proclivities and every chance he got he would kill deer, even in the moonlight from the window of his own parlour. To be rid of him, Mr Ellice gave him a sum of money and sent him and his large family to Canada. His wife died there and leaving his family in that country, he came back to Strathspey. His two brothers, Mr Ellice sent to school and

afterwards got them situations in the excise. The old man was sent to Braemar, his native country, and thereafter peace reigned...... About Christmas 1844, my father met with tracks of men and dogs in the forest chasing the deer and found one that had been killed hidden away (Collie, 1908)

William Collie even turned to poaching himself in order to stock the estate with deer c1845:

On Sundays I would go three or four miles up the streams trout fishing, or else into the Mar and Atholl forests in search of young fawns. I could get £1 for every young fawn brought home alive. They were poached and I would be out all night for them. My father was the first who reared fawns on cow's milk and that is how Glenfeshie forest was at first stocked.

*The Deerstalker* c1831 – The Royal Collection. A woodcut which is thought to have been a study for Landseers painting *Poachers Deerstalking*

R*eturn from Deerstalking,* 1827 – from the Collection of the Duke of Northumberland.
The two characters are thought to be Charles Mackintosh and Malcolm Clark from Glenfeshie.

The shooting lodge at Ruigh Fionntaig c1870, a photograph by AM Urquhart –
by kind permission of Grantown Museum

# 7. The Sporting Estate

During the first half of the 19th century there was a great transfer of Highland estates to new owners. The old order of Highland elite had been much more vulnerable to financial embarrassment than their peers in other regions and more and more of the hereditary chiefs had fallen into debt. Some invited criticism for living beyond their means and for careless mismanagement of their estates. For others the debt came about as a result of unsuccessful investments in the infrastructure of their estates; building roads and bridges, enclosure and drainage for example, and in the provision of relief for destitute tenancies during bad seasons. Debt had been a fact of life amongst most Highland proprietors in the 17th and 18th centuries. Much of the debt in the 19th century was inherited and a considerable amount of income was tied up in servicing the interest charges. In addition each estate was burdened with an array of annuities, life rents and portions for family members. It was usual to make allowances to younger sons and daughters and these had become unavoidable charges on an estate. For a time, in the period from 1790 to 1812, money had flooded into the Highlands as a result of spectacular increases in cattle prices, income from sheep farming, fishing and illicit distilling and landowners were able to survive by demanding higher rents from their tenants. But then, just as dramatically, the prosperity had ebbed away in the 1820s. The hereditary elite of Highland society were financially doomed and the great land sales of this period were one result of the economic crisis.

But the transfer of estates to new owners wasn't simply due to an increase in the number of estates which had come onto the market. The value of a property was to increase with the massive growth of sheep farming and the expansion of deer forests and many of the affluent classes of Victorian Britain saw a Highland property as an investment. But perhaps the main factor was the recognition of the sporting opportunities that the Highlands had to offer. From the early part of the 19th century it became fashionable for wealthy and aristocratic folk to take a hunting lodge for the autumn season in order to enjoy the shooting.

Colonel Thomas Thornton (1757-1823), perhaps influenced by his father, who had commanded a troop of cavalry at the Battle of Culloden, was one of the first to visit Badenoch. He was an eccentric squire from Yorkshire who made several trips from 1784. He stayed at Raitts on the north side of the River Spey, built his own house at Loch Alvie in 1789 and recorded his activities in a "game book" writing an account of his visits in 1804. His writings are mostly concerned with the minor details of his shooting but his dinners were obviously very significant! He describes an expedition when he travelled by pony across the Feshie and up to Carn Ban:

> At 12 o'clock we came to the first snow, depositing our champaign, lime, shrub, porter in one of the large snow drifts. We agreed to dine there. A portable cooker was produced and the moor-cock and ptarmigant which had been killed on the way up were prepared (Thornton, 1804).

In these early days the interest was for shooting birds; the OSA for Kingussie in 1792 reports that:

> The hills abound with game and are much frequented by sportsmen. Grouse and tarmagan are plenty. In some parts black-cock and wood-cock are also to be found, though these are more rare. In the most remote and unfrequented places there are a number of stags and roe deer.

In 1812 Glenfeshie was advertised for lease in the Inverness Courier:

> The forest of Glenfeshie in Badenoch consisting of 13,706 acres, the property of the Duke of Gordon, is adapted either for a summer grazing to black cattle or for shooting ground to a sportsman who might wish to preserve the tract for deer, moor game and ptarmigan, all of which abound in the adjoining hills and with which it would be abundantly stocked in a very short time, if carefully kept for this purpose.

For many visitors the most significant reason for purchasing a Highland estate seems to have been that it was fashionable to view the Highlands with a romantic eye. This romantic image of Scotland was encouraged by the novels of Sir Walter Scott. A new interest in nature and appreciation of the picturesque landscape began to be aroused. The wilderness of scenic beauty with its romantic, historical and legendary associations led to the Highlands becoming an area where it was possible to commune with nature and achieve spiritual renewal. For the fashionable the attractions of the Grand Tour on the Continent were replaced by a visit to the mountains and rivers of the Highlands.

From 1820 the pace of change in ownership of Highland estates quickened and over the next 40 years two-thirds of estates were to acquire new proprietors. Some families who had held extensive tracts of land for many generations disappeared from the scene and even those who managed to survive were forced into massive sales of parts of their heritage to maintain solvency. Almost three-quarters of the Highlands were acquired by a new breed of proprietor from outside the region. They were merchants, financiers, lawyers and industrialists from the Lowlands or from England, many of whom had made their fortunes in lucrative business overseas. They lavished expenditure on their estates and in the process helped to subsidise the local economy from the profits of trade in distant parts of the world. 28 deer forests were formed in the Highlands by 1839 and a further 16 in 1840 (Devine, 2006) as the region became a major centre for the physical sports of hunting, shooting and fishing. It was said that "as soon as a man has amassed a fortune his first desire was to buy or rent a deer forest in Scotland and there to gather his friends to enjoy his hospitality and sport".

The Highlands possessed the qualities of remoteness and isolation but new transport facilities guaranteed reasonably quick connections from the great urban centres of the south. Coach services had improved significantly, by 1836 it was said that "a person might dine in Edinburgh one day and breakfast in Inverness the next" and the invention of the ocean going paddle steamer also brought a reliable and regular transport system (Devine, 2006).

Robert Somers wrote in 1848:

> Before leaving the vicinity of the Grampians it may be well to glance for a few minutes at the deer forests of which this mountainous region is the centre and which after yielding to the advances of agriculture and civilisation are rapidly reverting. New "forests" are rising up like mushrooms, here you have the new forest of Glenfeshie. But in all cases the preparatory steps are the same. Whether the old forest is simply revived or whether the new regions are brought within the mystic circle for the first time the same devastation precedes the completion of the enterprise. Houses, roads, enclosures, cattle, men - are all extirpated by a word, in order that deer may enjoy the luxury of solitude and sportsmen monopolise the pleasures of the chase.... The clearances which have taken place within the last few years to make room for these new deer forests have made little noise, simply because they were clearances of sheep not of people (Somers, 1848).

The 4th Duke of Gordon died in 1827 leaving the family with a crippling debt of £500,000. The Gordon estates were put in the hands of Trustees and the 5th Duke was obliged to put much of his property on the market. Most of the Gordon properties in Badenoch and Lochaber were sold and many went as sporting estates but, by these sales, the Duke was able to retain other parts of his estate. Invereshie was bought by George Macpherson Grant in 1816 and in 1825 it was let to the Duke and Duchess of Bedford for the Autumn shooting season, one of the earliest estates in the area to be let for this purpose. The Bedfords were almost certainly influenced by the Duchess' love and knowledge of the region in which she had been born and brought up. Later, in 1842, the Highlands received the royal seal of approval with a visit from Queen Victoria who was to establish her own Highland retreat at Balmoral in 1848.

The Bedfords leased the Invereshie part of Glen Feshie from c1825, building a shooting lodge at Ruigh Fionntaig on the west side of the river. In 1830 they turned their attention to the east side of the glen and Ruigh Fionntaig was taken over by the Rt Hon Edward Ellice and General Balfour of Balbirnie. The "Glenfeshie Gamebook" of 1834 in the Edward Ellice Papers, National Library of Scotland, records that 1289 grouse, 144 ptarmigan and 20 black game were shot in 1834. In 1839, the numbers had risen to 1709 grouse and 150 ptarmigan. However in 1830 Edward Ellice converted the lease to a "deer forest" even though the number of deer taken at that time seems to have been very low; just four roe deer and two red deer in 1834.

Katherine Jane Balfour, General Balfour's daughter, married Mr Ellice's son and their son records that she was responsible for introducing the first "district tartan" to the Highlands. She acted as hostess for her father and his friends at Ruigh Fionntaig and was concerned because the ghillies did not have a tartan to wear. When the sheep had come to the glen the shepherds from the Borders had brought with them a woollen cream and bluish checked plaid, Miss Balfour added a red overcheck to the shepherd's plaid and it was adopted by the ghillies in 1836 (Scarlett, 1988). It was to lead to the many variations of colour and weave effects which we now know as District Checks.

The lodge at Ruigh Fionntaig appears in some Urquhart photographs of c1870 and is described in the OS name book as "chiefly of wood and used as a shooting lodge, they *(the buildings)* are one storey high, partly thatched and in good repair". In 1872-73 the Rt Hon Edward Horsman, MP, shooting tenant at the time, made many alterations, replacing the wooden buildings with stone structures which had slated roofs and adding stables, offices and venison and game larders (NRAS 771/Bundle 1470 and 1471). Ruigh Fionntaig was the principal shooting lodge until c1892 when the present Glenfeshie Lodge was built.

The main base for the Bedford parties was the Doune of Rothiemurchus which was leased from Patrick Grant. Georgina, Duchess of Bedford, was particularly fond of Glen Feshie and in 1830 she established a settlement or "lodge" at Ruigh Aiteachan on the east side of the river, seeing it as her own retreat and making regular visits there until her death in 1853. Margaret Gordon describes her father, the scientist Sir David Brewster, then residing at Belleville, being called on to attend the shooting parties:

> The late Duchess of Bedford, with her gay circle of fashion, of statesmen, artists, and lions of all kinds produced a constant social stir in which Sir David was frequently called to bear his part and he retained many lively recollections and anecdotes of the strange scenes and practical jokes of that "fast" circle (Gordon, 1870).

The Bedfords introduced the young painter, Edwin Landseer, to the Highlands and it was here, over the next three decades, that he was to find inspiration for some of his paintings. He was to paint many pictures of the deer, the life and the landscape. More accounts of these times appear in the chapter, "Georgina, Duchess of Bedford, Sir Edwin Landseer and "the Huts".

The "sporting scene" brought prosperity to the glen throughout the rest of the 19th century. Over the next decades the deer forests, along with the grouse moors, provided full time employment for many gamekeepers and stalkers. William Collie's father was employed as a keeper from the early days and William Collie himself spent his childhood in the glen and was later employed as a gamekeeper. During the later decades of the 19th century, the shooting estate was consolidated and improved by the Macpherson Grants. Fences were erected, tracks were constructed and a bridge built at Achleum, where another small lodge was built for the keeper. Shooting tenants would pay increasing sums to lease the estate

**The Archaeology of the Sporting Estate**

The three sites of Carnachuin, Ruigh Fionntaig and Ruigh Aiteachain were the main centres of activity for the sporting estate in the 19th century. Carnachuin, is marked in its present location on the Thomson map of 1830 and continues as the base for the present estate; most of the original features here have been destroyed. However at Ruigh Fionntaig the remains of several buildings of the stone lodge built in 1872-73 are seen. They replaced the original lodge of 10 buildings depicted on the 1st Edition OS map of 1869.

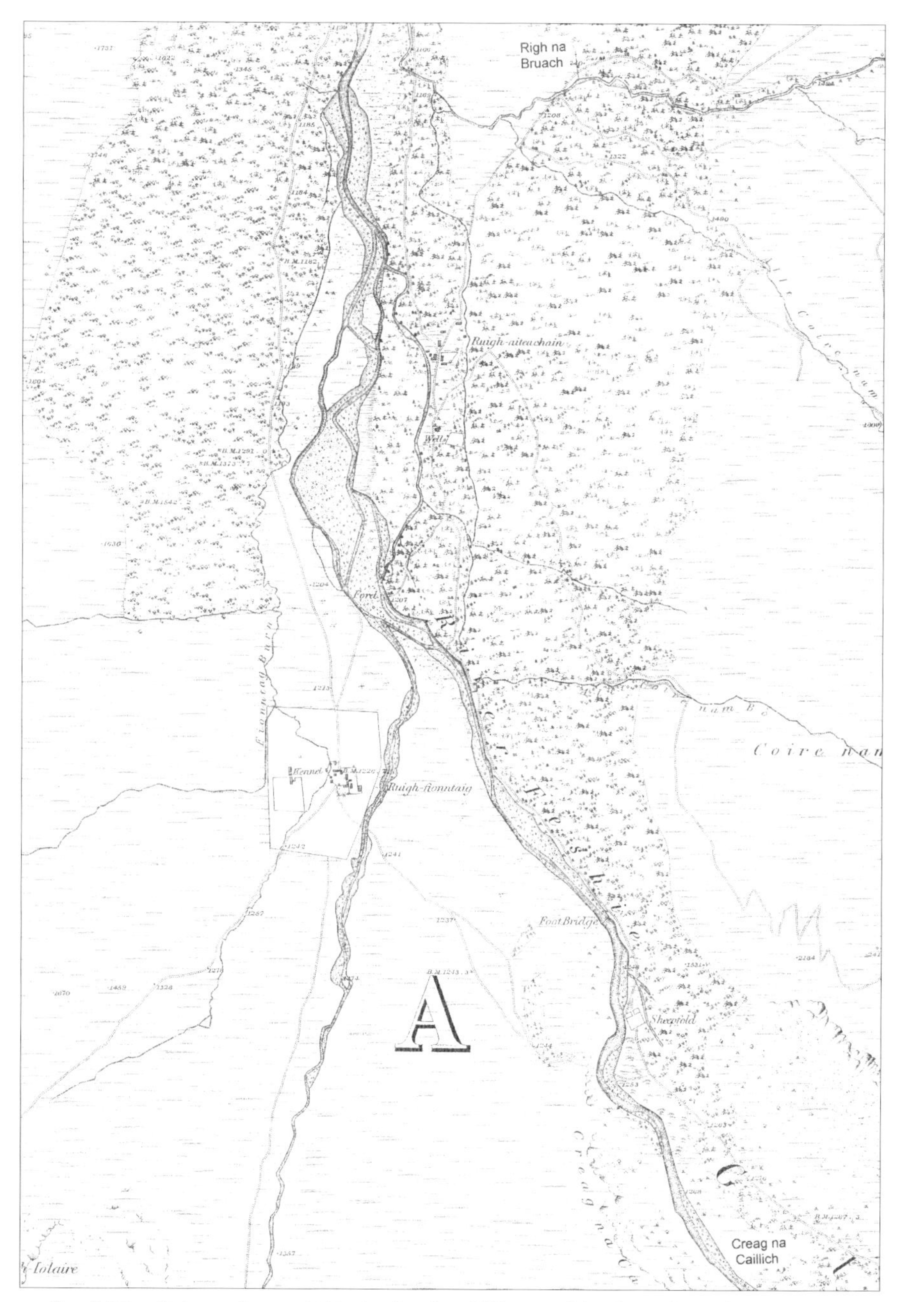


First Edition Ordnance Survey, 1869, showing the middle part of the glen with Ruigh Fionntaig and Ruigh Aiteachan. The settlements of Righ na Bruach and Creag na Caillich have been annotated.

On the east side of the river, at Ruigh Aiteachan, there is one roofed bothy maintained by the Mountain Bothies Association and the remains of three other buildings, one of which has a prominent chimney "stalk". The 1st Edition OS survey of 1869 has 9 buildings in two groups and the OS name book of the same year describes them as "a number of houses one storey in height and partly of wood, those of stone are thatched and the whole are in good repair". Contemporary accounts, paintings and photographs confirm the south group of buildings as "The Duchess of Bedfords Huts" and they are seen in a splendid set of Urquhart photographs of c1870. Today the standing chimney which is 5m in height is all that remains of these huts; most of them have been destroyed by the construction of a track.

The chimney has an interesting history. In the heyday of the Bedfords tenancy it had been decorated with deer frescoes by Sir Edwin Landseer. As the building decayed the frescoes inevitably suffered but, following her visit to the glen in 1860, Queen Victoria, a great lover of Landseer's work, requested that a timber building be erected around the chimney to protect the frescoes. This later building was still standing in the 1930s but was destroyed by a falling tree in the 1950s. Today there is evidence of a timber building surrounding the chimney and the remains of the fallen tree nearby. The site at Ruigh Aiteachan is considered in more detail in the chapter, "Georgina, Duchess of Bedford, Sir Edwin Landseer and the Huts".

Houses for the gamekeepers and the watchers who maintained the sporting estate were built at a number of sites on the estate. A valuation of buildings in 1853 (NAS GD176/1463/3/1) refers to a deer foresters house with byre, stables and kennels at Ruinabruich *(Righ na Bruach)* and a ruined deer watchers house at Auchercoit *(Achleum-a-choid)*. A small lodge is marked on the 1903 2nd Edition of the OS map 800m to the north of the ruins of the old township of Achleum-a-choid, it was probably built c1890, the same time as the present Glenfeshie Lodge, when a considerable number of upgrades, among them the "pony" bridge at Achleum, were made.

The bridge at Carnachuin is thought to have been first erected across the river in the 1870s; it saw many reinforcements, not least by the Canadian Foresters during WW2, before finally being washed away in the spate of September 2009. Throughout the upper glen there are the wasted remains of well-constructed "stalkers" paths. One of the paths ascends the Slochd Beag and the Allt Lorgaidh to its upper reaches where there are the remains of small shelters most likely connected with the deer stalking. Another ascends the shoulder of Druim nam Bo above Ruigh Aiteachan and yet another, built c1892 and known as the "pony path", ascends Choire Fhearnagan to Carn Ban Mor from the bridge at Achleum.

## 8. William Collie's Story

William Collie was born at Dalnavert in 1829 and spent his early life in Glen Feshie. He wrote his memoirs in later life and has given an insight into the working life of an employee on a sporting estate in those early days:

> In 1833, Glenfeshie was made a forest by the Hon Edward Ellice MP and my father was appointed head forester....In 1837 we all went to the Glen (Carn a Chunie house). Robert my brother was assistant footman at the lodge and Duncan was kennel boy. I was then only eight years old and only did light work. Father was then 43 years of age. He retained his situation until advancing years compelled him, in 1855, to cease work. During this time my duties were closely associated with his. *(Peter Collie and his family of five children are noted as being resident at Carnachuin in the 1851 census)*
>
> My first steady employment was as a ladies gillie, leading them on ponies through the hills. At twelve I worked the croft of five acres and could plough better then than I could at twenty. I was badly situated for school. There was a parochial school open during the winter three or four miles away. During the winter of 1843-44 when living at Dalnavert I attended the Laganlia School, where we had an excellent teacher. I also went to dancing school and became adept at the Highland fling, hornpipe, triple bar, sword dance and all the rest of it....... In 1843, at the age of 14, I was the dogman going to the forest every day during the season, leading staghounds and slipping them after wounded deer. I had the position for four years, in the fifth I had always to accompany my father as his eyes were giving way........ At 15 I took on a contract supplying the various lodges with peat fuel. My father helped me in this, cutting and stacking the peat after it had dried, I employed about 15 men and girls. The contract amounted to £60 or £70 which was considered a large sum in those days. Strong active full grown girls were paid only 10d a day and lads or men from 18 years upwards, who did double the work that would be done nowadays got from 1s to 1s 3d a day. I continued at this occupation until I was 19 and all the time gave every penny of my earnings to my father.........
>
> We are now in the year 1848 and during the five preceding years no young man worked harder or suffered more fatigue. I had contracts for making and improving the road to the peat moss at a very low figure and almost killed myself to make the common wages of the day. Rising every day at 2am I walked three miles to work, my dinner consisting of a handful of oatmeal to be made into brose with butter or treacle. Often, as it was impossible to light a fire, I was forced to make the brose with cold water, yet ate it with relish. There was never any scarcity of food in our house, but Scotland's fare was frugal in those days. The daily fare usually was porridge and milk for breakfast, potatoes and milk, soup, or fish for dinner, gruel or "brochan" for supper and a man living on that food would do more work than two perform nowaday........The hardships I suffered during the

time I was a gillie in the Glenfeshie forest are almost indescribable. My father could stalk but he had no knowledge of managing or working a forest and I had to learn everything by practical experience and hard work. He was always strong and hardy and had very little sympathy for others far less me. His main object always was to get near a deer and see it killed. I had to manage the gillies and ponies by signals so as to have them near in the event of a kill; and had always to lead a pair of staghounds home and often to carry a rifle. Our house was two miles from the huts or shooting boxes as they were often called.......... After breakfast I would start out at 6am with the gillies on a 6 mile walk along a bridle path. My father and the gentlemen stalkers would overtake us riding and the spying, stalking and chasing would continue on until dark. When there was a kill or chase we would not get back to the huts before 10 or 12 at night, worn out and so hungry as to be ready to eat anything. In the matter of food the hounds were as well cared for as human beings and their porridge was just as clean as if it had been prepared for our own consumption. After attending to the dogs I had to walk home a distance of two miles and next morning at 6am would be off again with a fresh gentleman........... Rifles were very scarce in those days. I never had one when chasing wounded deer with dogs and only those who have been at the game know how dangerous it is to stick a stag attacked by hounds. Only experts and experienced men can do it and they only at great risk to themselves. In six years I saw several dogs killed and had various narrow escapes myself.

In 1849 there were a great many changes. The Duchess of Bedford converted Rothiemurchus into a forest for her son, Lord Alexander Russell. She transferred my uncle, Robert, who had been her forester in Glenfeshie, to Rothiemurchus and Lord Alexander who left with his regiment for Canada asked the Duchess to put me in his place. The Duke of Leeds took a lease of the Invereshie forest and my father retired. The Duchess sent for me and said "Well, Lord Alexander before he left, asked me to give the charge of the forest here to you. I am about to send your uncle to our Rothiemurchus forest". I was for the moment stupefied and am not sure that I even said "thank you" as my special ambition was to aspire to the Invereshie forest and its sudden and unexpected realisation seemed almost to stun me. The Duchess continued "I told Lord Alexander that I thought you were much too young for such a charge, but I see you are not much elated and hope he will not be disappointed by you". Next day I heard the Duke was taking his head man and a lot of others from Braemar......... In October of that year the Duchess of Bedford engaged me as her forester and being only 19 years of age was the youngest man known ever to get charge of a deer forest. The house was not clear for me to reside in until 1849 when my father, mother and family moved into it from Carnachuine.

Miss Ann Rose, my future wife, was at the period staying at the Duchess' gardener's house and having fallen in love with her the whole world was therefore smooth sailing. The Duchess became very fond of her and was delighted when she heard that her young forester and her favourite had got together........ The first season I was more successful in the forest than my uncle had ever been and one and all were pleased. The Duchess told me she was pleased to send a good report to Canada, but that was the last I saw of the noble lady. In April 1852, the Duchess went to Italy for her health and in May sent from Venice a very pretty and costly trousseau, wishing us all manner of happiness. The good and noble Duchess died in that year shortly after our marriage and out of respect for her memory there was no deer stalking during the season.

In 1853 the Duke of Leeds who leased the forest of Invereshie added the forest of Glenfeshie and the fates were against me. I was reduced to the position of under-forester and had to live in a bothy for 2 months during the stalking season. In 1854 I gave in my resignation to the Duke of Leeds. There came an immediate reply: "I am extremely sorry to lose such a promising young man. No man could be more highly recommended than he has been by Lord Alexander, Mr Romilly and Sir Edwin Landseer, independently of the high opinion I myself have formed."

William Collie and his family left Glenfeshie and boarded a ship in Liverpool bound for Australia. Unfortunately, before reaching Ireland and Cork harbour, it was discovered that there was cholera on board. The family took refuge on the top galley of the ship and survived without food in the cold and rain for six days before the ship returned to Liverpool and quarantine. During this time 87 people had died.

William Collie was in a difficult situation, under no circumstances was he going to go back on board the ship and therefore the passage money had to be forfeited. The Duke of Leeds came to his rescue and the family found themselves back in Glenfeshie where eventually William Collie was engaged to go to Coulin in Loch Carron to open up a new deer forest.

*Georgina, Duchess of Bedford,* 1823 -
© The British Library Board

*Edwin Landseer,* by Sir Francis Grant -
© National Portrait Gallery, London

Landseer's well known *Monarch of the Glen,* painted in 1851 -
© by kind permission of Diageo, on loan to the National Museums Scotland.

# 9. Georgina, Duchess of Bedford, Sir Edwin Landseer and "The Huts"

Georgina, Duchess of Bedford (1781-1853) was the youngest daughter of the 4th Duke and Duchess of Gordon. She was born and brought up at Gordon Castle, near Fochabers. Her life-long association with the area of Badenoch and Strathspey started through her mother's love and interest in the estate of Kinrara, a few miles to the north of Glen Feshie on the north side of the River Spey. Her mother, Jane, Duchess of Gordon, was to settle and make improvements to the estate following her separation from the Duke in the late 1780s. Duchess Jane was a warm hearted, energetic and vivacious lady who was to secure good matches for all of her five daughters. In 1803 Georgina married the much older Duke of Bedford, a prominent and influential aristocrat. It was his second marriage and they were to have 10 surviving children.

In 1823 John, Duke of Bedford (1766 – 1839) had become the patron of the young Edwin Landseer (1802-1873) and in 1824 he introduced the painter to the Highlands. The Bedfords leased Glen Feshie for the autumn shooting season from c1825 and Landseer was to find inspiration for many pictures there. He painted his patrons and their family, the landscape and the people, but was particularly fond of portraying the animals. Some of Landseers' most notable works are in Glen Feshie - "Return from Deerstalking" and "Waiting for the Deer to Rise" figure Charles Mackintosh and Malcolm Clark who were gamekeepers in the glen at the time. The settlement of Ruigh Aiteachan is known to have been associated with Landseer and he was to decorate some of the chimney pieces with frescoes of deer.

The Duke and Duchess of Bedford made annual visits to Scotland from 1825. Georgina and Landseer became "intimate" friends, almost certainly lovers and inevitably Glen Feshie figured prominently in their relationship, which was to last until her death in 1853. It is generally accepted that Landseer was the father of the youngest of Georgina's ten children, Lady Rachel Russell, who was born in June 1826. The "menage a trois" seems to have progressed quite happily over the years. The devotion of the Duke and Duchess to each other never wavered, although both had close relationships with others of the opposite sex. The Duchess, is said to have had a very warm hearted, exuberant and charismatic personality. Sarah Murray of Kensington writes of meeting her on a walk at Loch an Eilean in 1801:

> Lady Georgina was at some distance from her mother and on seeing us, came bounding from rock to rock, so light and airy. I fancied her elegance personified. (Murray of Kensington, 1799)

And Charles Fraser Mackintosh has:

> *(Georgina was)* the steady close friend and protector of all poor people far and near and her name to this day is deservedly held in warmest affection (Fraser Mackintosh, 1897)

The Bedfords built a shooting lodge at Ruigh Fionntaig at some point before 1828 when it is marked on a Telford plan. A single building appears in a Landseer painting, c1830, at the location. But from 1830 the Bedfords turned their attention to the east side of the river which they leased from the Mackintosh of Mackintosh and the west side of the river was taken over by Edward Ellice and General Balfour of Balbirnie. The Bedfords main residence for the Autumn seasons was the Doune of Rothiemurchus but the Duchess, who was particularly fond of the Glen Feshie, established a settlement, or "Huts" as they were known, at Ruigh Aiteachan. She wrote a letter in 1838 to Mackintosh of Mackintosh:

> I now enclose a draft for the shooting at Kincraig and Glen Feshie. I hope next year to see you there and show you what a little paradise I have in that lovely Glen, as I flatter myself I improve it every year (NAS GD176/2226).

And in 1839, also to "the Mackintosh", she deplores the cutting down of trees to make a track:

> I grieved over the track made amongst your beautiful trees - it is a sad pity, as it gives a look of desolation to a lovely spot (NAS GD176/2230).

Many distinguished guests were invited to join the shooting parties at Ruigh Aiteachan. Charles Tankerville, Viscount Ossulston, has written an account of his visit in 1833. Of the huts he writes:

> Nothing could be more picturesque than the spot chosen by this little colony for their autumn retreat. A cluster of pretty cottages on the broad lawn of grass, surrounded by this fine forest of Rothiemurchus of self sown firs, some of remarkable size and weird form, with acres of tall junipers grouped about, as only nature can group, in these natural lawns of grass. Every here and there they opened out into beautiful vistas showing the bonny hills of Mar - "Binoch and Scarsoch" where many a wandering deer is feeding. We made for the principal building and there found them at lunch. The old Duke was sitting with an umbrella over his head, to save his soup from being watered by a dribble which was leaking from the roof above; quite happy and resigned to his fate - a wet seat in a wooden cabin instead of Woburn Abbey (Tankerville, 1891).

And Charles Mathews describes the "Huts" when writing to his mother in 1833:

> I was immediately conducted to view the habitation, and certainly never saw anything half so original in its conception or so perfect in execution as the whole thing. The appearance was that of a small Indian settlement, consisting of one low building containing three or four bedrooms and the kitchen etc and two smaller ones of one room each, the one being dining room, parlour, drawing room, and hall and the other containing two beds for ladies. The rest of the settlement was composed of tents, various in size and in use. The buildings themselves looked like the poorest peasant cottages. The walls (were) made of turf and overgrown with foxglove and the roof of untrimmed spars of birch. The apartments within corresponded perfectly with their exterior; everything of rough unpeeled birch. The fires of peat and fir blazed away upon the ground, in short, everything bespeaking the habitation of some tasteful wood-cutter. The drawing room was of tolerable length and height, but the bedrooms only just large enough to turn round in. The beds of the ladies resembled small presses or chests of drawers, with

*Deerstalking in the Highlands,* 1828 - the Duchess of Bedford, her brother, the Duke of Gordon and her youngest son, Alexander Russell - © National Gallery of Scotland

*The Naughty Child,* 1834 – thought to be the Duchess of Bedford's youngest daughter, Lady Rachel Russell – V & A Images/Victoria and Albert Museum

mattresses stuffed with heather and pillows of the same let into them like hammocks of a vessel. The gentlemen's apartments were in tents, each containing two small heather couches, side by side on tressels, one small table and a wash-hand-stand and foot-bath, but no chairs, curtains nor looking-glass. The carpet was of turf, upon which our wardrobes were arranged, protected by pieces of wood in case of promiscuous or superfluous damp (Dickens, 1879).

Later Charles Fraser Mackintosh wrote:

The place which Lady Georgina Gordon, Duchess of Bedford, was so fond of, sometimes called "The Island", sometimes "Georgina", was the favourite residence, and her "huts" were visited by the highest in Great Britain....... Mrs Fraser, a favourite servant with the Duchess, has often told me that the Duchess was in the habit of saying that she loved her huts in Glenfeshie over and above every spot in the world. The huts were mere turf walls, bottomed with stone and over each door rowans were planted and trained, carrying out the ancient view that kept away the witches. Above the fireplace in the dining-room hut, was a fine picture of a stag on rough plaster by Sir Edwin Landseer. The whole needed greatest care from the severity of winter weather (Fraser Mackintosh, 1897).

Perhaps Georgina was intent on recreating a memory from her childhood. Elizabeth Grant describes an episode at Kinrara in Georgina's early life:

She *(Georgina's mother, Jane)* had for the last few years spent her summers at a little farm on the Badenoch property...... the real old farmhouse of Kinrara, where she was happier and more agreeable and the society she gathered round her far pleasanter....... It was a sort of backwoods life, charming to young people amid such scenery. In the but and ben, constituting the small farm cabin, it was she and her daughter the Lady Georgina dwelt in, by the help of white calico, a little white wash, a little paint and plenty of flowers they made their apartment quite pretty.........half the London world of fashion, all the clever people that could be hunted out from all parts, all the north country, all the neighbourhood from far and near without regard to wealth or station, and all the kith and kin both of Gordons and Maxwells flocked to this encampment in the wilderness during the fine autumns to enjoy the free life, the pure air, and the wit and fun the Duchess brought with her to the mountains (Grant, 1898) .

Charles Tankerville was to form a lifelong friendship with Landseer; he describes his first meeting with the painter:

The next morning I was sent off to try my luck with the old forester Charlie Mackintosh who in his early days had been a poacher of the first order. So astute and active in limb was he that none of the foresters of Mar and Atholl could ever catch him. On arriving at our ground and taking a view with the glass we saw a large herd of hinds with a big stag, grazing towards the burn. We forthwith prepared by a quick stalk to cut in before them when suddenly they started and the well known crack of a rifle denoting that someone was there before us. "It'll be a poacher" said Charlie. We ensconced ourselves behind a heathery knoll

*Glenfishie Houses* – thought to be the huts at Ruigh Aiteachan –
© National Library of Scotland (GB233/MS 15152)

*The Duchess of Bedford's Dining Bothie at Glenfeshie,* 1833, by Charles Mathews –
by kind permission of the Duke of Bedford and the Trustees of the Bedford Estates

*The Duchess of Bedford's Hutts,* viewed from the south – a photograph c1870 by AM Urquhart - reproduced by kind permission of Grantown Museum

*The Duchess of Bedford's Hutts,* viewed from the west – a photograph c1870 by AM Urquhart - reproduced by kind permission of Grantown Museum

> within a few yards of our poacher, to watch his proceedings before we finally pounced upon him. He was busy employed in grallocking *(disembowelling)* his deer. This he did with great quickness and dexterity, not omitting to wash the tallow and other treasures carefully in the burn and deposit them carefully on a stone beside the deer. He next let the head hang over, so as to display the horns, and then, squatting down on a stone opposite, took out of his pocket what I thought would be his pipe or his whisky flask; but it was a sketch-book!........... Seeing that we had mistaken our man, I came out into the open and found myself face to face with my friend of many years to come - Landseer. He was staying with the Duke and Duchess of Bedford in their little settlement of wooden houses on the other side of the Fishie. It was arranged that I should go over to lunch there the next day (Tankerville, 1891).

And later at the end of the 1833 visit, Tankerville invites Landseer back to Chillingham:

> It is difficult to do justice to the attractions of his society. He was acknowledged to be the best company of his day. His powers of description, whether of people or scenery were most graphic and amusing and though simple in words, had very much of natural poetry about them. And his anecdotes which were full of humour, the marvellous changes of voice and expression of countenance he could assume as a perfect actor brought the person themselves in reality before you. Even in the common occurrences of a daily walk he would draw ones attention to something curious or absurd which one might have passed 50 times without noticing. With this pleasant companion I had less regret at leaving our happy quarters. But still it was a sad moment when we saw the last of Glenfishie and its charming belongings (Tankerville, 1891).

Charles Mathews describes a journey from the Doune to the "Huts":

> ...... preparations were made for the flitting from the Doune to take up residence in a romantic glen about 15 miles off where the Duchess loves to dwell. Orders were given that all grande toilette should be suspended until further notice and that those who were not prepared to rough it should remain behind. Leaving the ladies to get there their own way we gentlemen at break of day set off on our shaggy ponies with the intention of shooting our way over the mountain tops to the glen. After a most fatiguing ascent, we reached the ptarmigan hills where the party dispersed in various directions in quest of game. Having ascertained the direction of the glen I left them and proceeded alone across the mountains with the day before me to enjoy the magnificent views which presented themselves on all sides. After a most delightful walk I entered the narrow pass leading to the glen, through the centre of which foamed and tumbled the river Fishie, forming in its course an endless variety of waterfalls. Towards evening, having waded four or five times up to my middle through the stream, I entered that part of the pass which is called *par excellence* "the" glen. There I found the ladies. The Duchess, Lady Rachel, and the maids had arrived before me in their tilt-cart; Miss Balfour and Lady Georgina having, under the escort of a guide, walked all the way from the Doune (Dickens, 1879)

Charles Mathews seems to have enjoyed himself immensely. In a letter, again to his mother, he writes:

> There is no moment which can be found for long letter writing. I have been living for the last four days in a tent and am in a state of excitement. I cannot sit down. Everything here is wild, the country is wild, the weather is wild, the two young ladies who are here are wild as March hares and I verily believe if I stay another week here I shall be wild myself. Which you will the more easily believe as you, who know me better than anybody in the world, never gave me credit for much sense........Here we have been now above a week, living on venison, grouse, hares, partridges, black-cock, ptarmigan, plovers, salmon, char, pike, trout, beef, mutton, pork etc. etc, all killed by ourselves and nearly on the spot, at any rate within a mile of the house. The ladies have only the dress of the country shape and material; bedgown of some light material, generally striped, a blue cloth or grey stuff petticoat, very short, scarlet, blue and grey stockings, aprons and mittens and snoods of red or blue through their hair and coloured handkerchiefs protect their heads from rain and wind, but bonnets are unknown. The gentlemen wear the kilts and everything is picturesque in the extreme. It is without any exception the most delightful sort of life I have ever seen or experienced. Amusements of every sort are constantly going on. The guitar is in great request and a small piano of two octaves, made for travelling is constantly going. Lord Ossulston and Miss Balfour both sing beautifully and we get up songs and trios without end. A more charming spot for midnight serenading cannot be imagined. The weather has been very rough and stormy since our sojourn in the glen and sketching and painting have been out of the question. The party is much too full of fun to allow anything like study to go on and even if that were not the case painting is impossible in our present dwelling (Dickens, 1879).

Mathews describes a visit to dine with Edward Ellice at Ruigh Fionntaig:

> On the other side of the Fishie, about a quarter of a mile from us, is another far inferior dwelling, formerly occupied by the Duchess, and now the residence of Captain Ross, Mr Ellis and his son. They have taken the shooting ground which joins that of Rothiemurchus and are capital neighbours. Our party went on Monday to dine with them. One of our tents was sent across to form a banqueting hall and each man took his knife and fork with him. The day turned out tremendous. Torrents of rain and tempests of wind succeeded each other till we began to fear that the river would be too swollen to allow us to attempt the fords. At seven o'clock however in the midst of a hurricane we set off. The tilt-cart held six and the rest were accommodated on ponies. The cart, not particularly easy in itself, threatening to be upset at any moment, the water tearing down with great rapidity and filling the bottom of the cart and the wind with the most frightful gusts positively rocking it to and fro. On the other side we were met by the piper who walked before us to the house with half a dozen gillies in procession on each side of the cart. On reaching the Wooden House, anticipating rather uneasy quarters in the tent, we were most agreeably surprised by finding that the idea had

*The Duchess of Bedford on a pony* c1833 –
Private collection

*Arrival at the ball at Glenfeshie* c1833 –
Private collection

*Reception at Glenfeshie with Edward Ellice,*
*the Duchess of Bedford and others 1833* –
Private collection

been abandoned and that Ellis's bedroom had been cleared out, beds removed and guns unshipped to form a dining room. A tremendous fire of wood and peat blazed upon the hearth and a long well-secured table stood in the middle of the room, well covered with candles of wax stuck in turnip candlesticks of the most elegant workmanship. On the timbers of the roof other similar candlesticks were fixed, so that illumination was splendid. The banquet was profuse and the dressing exquisite. Venison in every shape and disguise, wild game and fish of every sort and description, ending with cranberry and blueberry tarts and all sorts of clotted cream, custards, apple puddings and turnip pies. Lots of champagne, claret, moselle, ices &c were disposed of. The feast was exceedingly gay, the piper playing all the time outside and an enormous bonfire of birch and fir trees kept constantly alive in spite of the most tremendous unceasing hurricane which raged without. After the ladies retired, mulled claret and whiskey toddy were introduced, and coffee and tea with songs and choruses welcomed their return. All these things having been duly honoured, gillies were despatched to see in what state the river was, as it was strongly suspected that it might have increased so as to prevent our return. The report justified an attempt - though not a thing to be done without great hazard in consequence of the darkness of the night, the rapidity of the torrent and the hurricane which raged. The tilt cart was brought out and the ladies and boys packed within it, the gentlemen mounted their ponies and our host ordered out their horses to escort the party. All being in order the cavalcade set out, preceded by a dozen gillies bearing immense blazing firebrands of fir branches, next the pipes playing lustily before the tilt cart which rocked about through the mud and moss most alarmingly, followed by the horsemen and a second detachment of blazing branches. The effect was very fine indeed and the commanding figure of Ross in his Scotch bonnet, large smugglers jacket, bare legs and tartan hose, mounted on a large black charger, who rode in front of the whole party completed the procession. In spite of all the difficulties we reached our own quarters in safety and within our tents for the night, many were the glasses of whiskey toddy, and pipes and cigars which were consumed by the survivors. Our tent was anything but lulling in the course of the night but a fine sunshiny morning put to flight the terrors of the past night (Dickens, 1879).

Charles Mathews describes a ball which was thrown for the neighbourhood:

The night after the dinner-party we gave a ball and all the lads and lasses in the neighbourhood (that is about a dozen in all, being the population of 10 or 12 miles around) were invited. Two fiddlers and a piper worked away from eight in the evening till six in the morning, when the delicate young ladies who had walked ten miles to the ball in the rain and waded through three fords on their way, set out again after dancing all night to walk back ten miles to their work. The quantity of whiskey toddy drank upon the occasion you may suppose was not small, but there was no one, I understand very fou. The Duchess, notwithstanding a slight failing, from a previous accident, in her knee, danced as well as anyone of the party and in the reels decidedly beat all. The young ladies are sylphs. As to myself, I must own I am amazed. The manner in which I walk over the hills, ford rivers, scale rocks and dance reels is past belief. I feel just as strong and able to support fatigue as I ever was in my life and the more I take the stronger I am. Post-time has come and so I must leave off, hardly knowing what I have said, but you must make allowances for writing on a dark blowing day, in a small room with 16 people in it all talking at the same time (Dickens, 1879).

Perhaps one of the most daring and enterprising expeditions was a visit to Loch Avon in 1833. Charles Tankerville writes:

It was unanimously proposed by the ladies and gentlemen to make an expedition to the top of Ben Avon, the highest peak in the Cairngorms, from which a magnificent view of all these mountains is to be seen. A singular feature in the mountain we are about to explore is a very beautiful lake near its summit. Black precipices of porphyry and granite spring up sheer from its sides, straight like plummet lines from its waters edge till they reach the highest tops. From this lake which is on the water shed of this range the river Avon takes its source....... As the time required for our expedition would be too long for us to return the same day, it was determined to take a tent for the ladies to bivouac in by the side of the lake and the gentlemen were to take up their quarters for the night in the Poachers Cave which is amongst the boulders heaped like an avalanche from the peaks above....... Early the following morning our party was mustered at the principal house of our little settlement. We had all assembled there for breakfast and found the five ponies which were provided for the Duchess and her two daughters and two of her friends already at the door with a gillie in attendance upon each. We gentlemen with a good staff in our hands trusted to our legs for safe conveyance. We made up the party with two good men, Sir Edwin Landseer and Charles Mathews, also the cheery companion of my travels. Mathews, who was then beginning his career as an architect, already gave evidence of the talents which brought him afterwards into such notoriety as an actor. He amused but rather startled us by appearing in a smart tartan kilt with all the appointments of a Highlander.

So the party set forward merrily through the old pine woods, where the path gradually wound its way above the base of the hill, till we came out into the open. Here the weather-beaten trees, thinly scattered were stunted and torn by the blasts but the profusion of cranberries and blooming heather made up for this defect and the ladies promised us a feast of puddings and tarts when our days work was over....... At last we were coming to the real tug of war, as the view opened out into a higher region of precipitous rocks and landslips. The spur of the hill along which we were climbing by a zig-zag path of rolling stones seemed the only practicable pass up the mountain. But, setting our faces to it we plodded on and after a long pull and a stop for breath and for luncheon in a panorama of the finest mountain scenery in these parts, we arrived at our destination on the plateau above, where the lovely lake lay before us, the bright sun giving splendid reflection of the peaks of Ben Avon frowning over it.

*Encampment at Loch Avon,* 1833 – untraced

*Loch Avon and the Cairngorm Mountains,* c1833 - © Tate, London 2011

Our first care was to choose a snug hollow to pitch our tents sheltered by high rocks. As a little breeze was springing up, we thought that a dish of char would be a welcome addition to our dinner and we made our way with our rods to the shore, leaving our men to fix the tents and light a fire and the ladies to fill a cauldron with the mysterious ingredients of a Scotch hodge-podge. On returning to our encampment we passed a charming evening. We grouped ourselves round the fire and its cauldron and of course the first act of the play was to discuss its contents and the char which were delicious. We afterwards spent a pleasant hour or two in singing some of the touching Scotch ballads and glees, for all the party was musical and there were some very good voices among them. The Highlanders, who love their national songs, gathered round to listen and the blaze of the fire upon the group made quite a pretty picture. The pipes then struck up and the men forthwith threw themselves into a wild Houlikin. We were in the country of the Strathspey, famed for its dancers, and the Strathspey step is neater and more elegant than the ordinary Highland fling. The piercing pipes and glare of the fire must have scared the deer for many a mile...... It was time to take ourselves to our perch for the night amongst the rocks. The night had closed in dark so we took a man with a lantern to light us over the slippery boulders. The slumbers of the party, under difficulties, were light and we made an early start next morning to return to the glen, bidding good-bye to one of the most charming scenes that can be found in the Highlands (Tankerville, 1891).

*(What is described is not an ascent of Ben Avon, but of Ben Macdui, Ben Macdui is the highest mountain in the Cairngorms, and on the route from Glen Feshie to Loch Avon. The camp must have been beside Loch Avon with the gentlemen staying under the Shelter Stone.)*

In October 1839 the Duke of Bedford died in the Highlands. Edwin Landseer had been exhibiting his paintings annually at the Royal Academy and had been made an Academician by this time. Of the sad occasion he writes:

I can think of nothing correctly, but the melancholy time I passed at the Doune and the sad termination of our anxious watchings (Lennie, 1976)

The following year was a difficult one for Landseer; his mother died and Georgina rejected his proposal of marriage. He was devastated and suffered the first of the many breakdowns which were to mar the rest of his life. Landseer never married but appears to have been very popular with the ladies. Georgina and Landseer remained good friends and continued to make regular visits to the Highlands, Landseer building his own hut close to her settlement in Glen Feshie. They seem to have kept in regular contact until her death in Nice in 1853.

Charles Fraser Mackintosh writes:

After her death *(Georgina's)* both sides of the Feshie were rented by the same sporting tenants and the houses *(at Ruigh Fionntaig)* opposite the huts, being built of wood were dryer and consequently became the principal residence. The late Alexander Mackintosh, 26th of Mackintosh, was on such friendly terms with the Duchess that latterly no conditions were inserted into her leases, the result being that the huts fell into ruins, particularly in the time of the Duke of Leeds, over whom the Mackintoshes had no control (Fraser Mackintosh, 1897).

In 1853 a lease between the Duke of Leeds and "the Mackintosh" for the shootings of Glenfeshie proposed that:

the Mackintosh *(was)* to hand over the Huts, cottages and buildings .....in complete repair and the Duke of Leeds *(was)* to maintain them in that state and leave them so at the expiry of his lease (NAS GD176/1468/2/1).

At the same time a valuation of the buildings was undertaken:

the buildings are, in general, in a very dilapidated state, the roofs in particular are bad and some of the huts I consider to be scarcely habitable.......the value of the whole subjects as they now stand is £288.11.7 and the sum of £86.5/- is required to put them in a tenantable condition (NAS GD176/1468/3/1) .

It would appear that these repairs were never carried out even though the Duke of Leeds occupied the lands and by 1860, when Queen Victoria visited the glen, the Huts were in a poor state.

Landseer was very much a favourite of Queen Victoria. In 1837 he had been commissioned to paint the pets of the Royal Family and for the next 30 years he was to paint many portraits and scenes of the Royal Family during their visits to Balmoral. Queen Victoria has written a romantic account of a journey from Braemar to Badenoch through Glen Feshie in September 1860. Of Landseer and the "Huts" she writes:

Then we came upon a most lovely spot - the scene of all Landseers glory - and where there is a little encampment of wooden and turf huts, built by the late Duchess of Bedford; now no longer belonging to the family and alas! All falling into decay - among splendid fir-trees, the mountains rising abruptly from the sides of the valley. We were quite enchanted with the beauty of the view (Helps, 1868)..

And the following year, in October 1861, she made a similar journey:

The huts, surrounded by magnificent fir-trees and by quantities of juniper-bushes, looked lovelier than ever; we gazed with sorrow at their utter ruin. I felt what a delightful little encampment it must have been, and how enchanting to live in such a spot as this beautiful solitary wood in a glen surrounded by the high hills. We went into one of the huts to look at a fresco of stags of Landseer's over a chimney-piece. Grant, on a pony, led me through the Fishie at the foot of the farmhouses (Helps, 1868).

Charles Fraser Mackintosh reports that following Queen Victoria's visit:

the 27th Mackintosh authorised *(that)* the dining-room be restored as far as possible, and a pretty wooden hall of the finest Glenfeshie wood, with handsome windows, was erected with the old gable, on which was Sir Edwin Landseers picture, properly enclosed and incorporated (Fraser Mackintosh, 1897).

Other visitors were to write about the "Huts":

In this forest *(Glenfeshie)* Landseer painted many pictures, being especially fond of studying the deerhounds bred by old Malcolm Clark, the fox-hunter. At one period there were two sets of huts in the glen, in one of which Landseer painted

The "pretty wooden hall" surrounding the chimney at Ruigh Aiteachan, a photograph taken 1920-1930 - © Pete Moore collection, origins untraced

The chimney at Ruigh Aiteachan viewed from the north, note the remains of the tree that has fallen through the roof of the building

The chimney at Ruigh Aiteachan
viewed from the west

A photograph, c1930s, of the chimney showing
the degraded remains of the deer frescoes painted
by Landseer – The Scots Magazine, Vol XXX
1938-39 p425/Pete Moore Collection

A plan of the chimney –
note the two lines of roof flashing

a group of deer with a suspicious hind on the plaster above the fireplace; but as the huts came to be disused, this chalk drawing was left exposed to the damp and though the remains of it are still to be seen, they are in a very dilapidated condition. The other of these huts was for a long time occupied by Georgina, Duchess of Bedford, who was greatly attached to the place, and so much so that when The Mackintosh proposed to sell some of the pine wood, she purchased most of the finest trees and her mark consisting of a tablet with her coronet and initials may still be identifying on some of them, although, horrible to relate, many of these badges have been removed by tourist visitors to the glen (Grimble, 1901).

Campbell Lennie attributes the demise of the frescoes to a lack of co-operation between Macpherson Grant and "the Mackintosh":

The destruction of some valuable, if unconventionally sited, works of art was due in part to a typical demarcation feud between two fiery Highland lairds. Georgina had merely leased the land, the responsibility for which was now a matter of dispute between Macpherson Grant and "the Mackintosh". Meantime the rising damp and the leaking roofs were eating at Landseers frescoes....... The cartoons were probably not as remarkable as those at Ardverikie; but their preservation might have been a matter of some concern, at least in a century which expressed almost unanimous praise for all Landseer's work. General Crealock was another who visited Georgina's "ghost village" long after its founder had been laid to rest

"The chief bothy where the Duchess had lived had had some charming drawings on its walls; but alas! When I was there, the place was in sad ruin, and but a few remnants of these pictures remained. In the hut which served as a dining room, however, there was one large drawing of a deer in good condition still, and fresh in colour - a charming sketch, and it was grievous to think that such a work of art was doomed to destruction, the more so as it might have been saved by removing it bodily from the wall"

Crealock, a fine amateur artist, did his best to preserve a record of the last large deer fresco by drawing a faithful copy *(untraced)* of it in 1892. The Ardverikie frescoes had been destroyed by fire; the loss of those in Glen Feshie was even more reprehensible. In 1954 a falling tree destroyed the last of Georgina's huts, exposing the final faint traces of Landseer's joyfully spontaneous wall-cartoons to the hungry Highland winds (Lennie, 1976).

Oral tradition has it that the bothy, now enclosed with "a pretty wooden hall of the finest Glenfeshie wood", was used as a church at the beginning of the 20th century but by the 1950s very little of Landseers frescoes on the chimney remained. Meta Scarlet writes regarding the old gable with the Landseer fresco:

My father took me to see it shortly after the war *(World War 2)* intending to show me the last of Landseer's murals but alas only rubble remained with faint tinges of colour on the plaster (Scarlett, 1988).

**The Location of "The Huts"**

The settlements established by the Bedfords have been referred to as "the Huts", "The Bedford Huts" and "The Duchess of Bedford's Huts" but their whereabouts has never been clearly identified. Three sites are put forward as candidates and it is quite possible that the different names refer to the different sites or that the three names are transferable between the three sites. It appears though that all three sites had some significance during the Bedford period. What follows is an attempt to "tie up" the archaeological evidence with the documentary and pictorial evidence and to work out a sequence of events.

The site of the shooting lodge at Ruigh Fionntaig, on the west bank of the river, is known by the present estate workers, as "The Bedford Huts" although Queen Victoria refers to it as the "Invereshie huts" in 1860-61. The "Duke of Bedford's Lodge" is marked on Telfords' plan of 1828 at this location and an early Landseer painting, "Glenfishie c1830-1835" (page 12), has a single building which is almost certainly the first lodge. Charles Tankerville describes his stay with Horatio Ross and his outing to the hills with "the old forester, Charlie Mackintosh" in 1833; Charles Mackintosh, gamekeeper, and his family are noted at Ruigh Fionntaig in the census of 1841. Charles Matthews, a guest of the Bedfords, tells the story of crossing the river in a tempestuous storm to dine with Edward Ellice at the shooting lodge *(of Ruigh Fionntaig)* in 1833. In 1863 Fraser Mackintosh refers to the buildings at Ruigh Fionntaig: "the houses opposite the huts *(of Ruigh Aiteachan)* being built of wood were dryer and consequently became the principal residence" and in 1869 the OS name book describes the buildings at Ruigh Fionntaig as "chiefly of wood and used as a shooting lodge". Urquhart photographs, c1870, of Ruigh Fionntaig show several wooden buildings of one storey height. But in 1872-73 the tenant at the time, the Rt Hon Edward Horsman MP, carried out extensive alterations which resulted in new buildings of dressed stone - stables, offices, a slaughter house and larders (NRAS 771, bundles 1470 and 1471); the stone footings of these buildings are clearly seen at the site today and have replaced the old settlement of wooden buildings.

Many contemporary descriptions, paintings and photographs confirm the settlement of Ruigh Aiteachan as the site of the "Duchess of Bedfords Huts". The 1841, 1851 and 1861 census records refer to Ruigh Aiteachan as "Eilenmore" or "Island" and Fraser Mackintosh in 1863 refers to the Duchess's favourite place in the glen as being called "The Island". Today it is hardly on an island but has a small stream on its east side running parallel to the River Feshie, making it more or less encircled by water. John Fraser, gamekeeper, and his wife Mary lived here in 1851; Mrs Fraser is described by Fraser Mackintosh in 1863 as a favourite servant of the Duchess. The couple had two daughters, Rachel born 1849, almost certainly named after Georgina's youngest child, and Georgina born 1853, without doubt named after Georgina herself.

A series of photographs taken in the 1870s by Alexander M Urquhart, of Grantown on Spey, and annotated "Duchess of Bedford's Hutts" has the buildings and the surrounding landscape concurring with the 1st Edition Ordnance Survey and several Landseer paintings are of scenes in the immediate vicinity, "Glenfeshie - also called Highland River, 1830-35" (page 17) for example, and "Scottish Landscape – Bringing in the Stag" (page 42), an early Landseer painting of 1830. In addition the buildings itemized in the builders valuation of 1853 (NAS GD176/1468/3/1) match those in the photographs

Today the site of Ruigh Aiteachan has a roofed stone bothy, the footings of two other buildings and the "footprint" of a building with an upstanding stone chimney. Without doubt the chimney piece was the one on which Landseer had painted the frescoes. A photograph of the badly deteriorating frescoes from the 1930s has the stonework matching. Two lines of flashing on the chimney provide evidence of two roofs. The upper line is seen on all faces of the chimney and, together with the "footprint" of a structure, indicate a building that has surrounded the chimney. This would have been "the pretty wooden hall of the finest Glenfeshie wood, with the old gable properly enclosed" which was constructed by the 27th Mackintosh. A photograph of c1930 shows a rather ornate wooden building overhung by a tree. We are told that the building was destroyed by a falling tree; today the remains of the tree lie within the "footprint" of the building. The archaeological evidence entirely fits the history of the building.

Two and a half kilometres to the south of Ruigh Aiteachan there is a further settlement of three buildings in the narrowest part of the glen, a particularly dramatic location. This settlement was named Creag na Caillich in the survey and is a bit of a mystery. All three buildings at the site seem to have been built to a plan; all have the substantial remains of stone and turf walls to a height c1m and all are on the same NW-SE alignment. Two of the buildings measure roughly 10 x 3m, whilst the third is 11 x 3.5m. This last is on a raised area, has two compartments and a wide entrance at the north gable end. No other features suggesting cultivation or farming activity are seen in the vicinity, indeed the site receives very little sunshine and is very much overshadowed by crags and trees. Strangely the settlement is not depicted on the 1st edition OS map of 1869 and no entries appear in the census records. The settlement would appear to fit the description of the Duchess of Bedford's huts given by Charles Mathews, (page 62), extremely well! Could these also be "The Duchess of Bedford's Huts" - the paradise she lovingly developed? Positive weight is given to the theory by two of Landseer's paintings; one shows the entrance of a hut which appears to be at the gable end of the building; it may be the entrance to the largest of the three buildings at this site which is also at the gable end. The other painting has the title "Hut at Glenfeshie" and shows a neglected turf bothy amongst trees; both these paintings indicate simple buildings of turf, quite unlike the buildings at Ruigh Aiteachan in the Urquhart photographs. In addition several other paintings by Landseer have been identified as scenes in the close neighbourhood of Creag na Caillich. It is quite probable that Georgina built this settlement too – could she have intended it to be a "shieling" settlement?

Creag na Caillich – the footings of the SE building

Creag na Caillich – the footings of the NW building

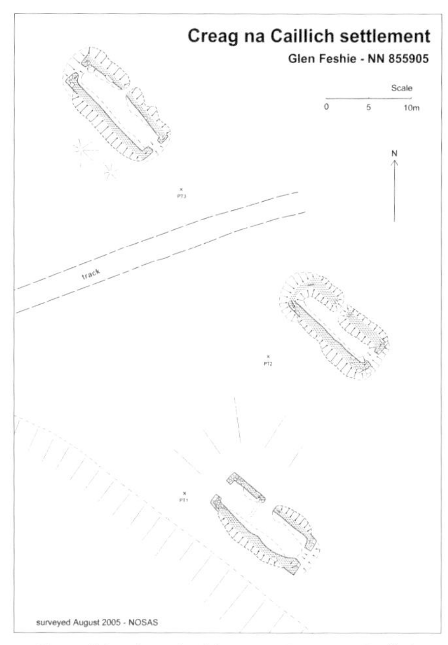


Plan of the three buildings at Creag na Caillich

*Exterior of the "Duchess of Bedford Hut"*, 1833 - © Philadelphia Museum of Art

*Hut at Glenfeshie* – courtesy of Sothebys

It is probable that all three of the sites were used by the Bedfords at some point in their 25 year association with the glen. The origin of the "shooting lodge" at Ruigh Fionntaig is not in doubt; it was established by the Duke. But it may be that by 1830, when he would have been 64 years of age, he had lost some of his interest for travelling every year, although he is mentioned as being at Ruigh Aiteachan in 1833. It seems that after 1830 it was the Duchess who pursued the lease of the east side of Glen Feshie and, perhaps intent on recreating the memories of her childhood at Kinrara, she established a simple settlement. But which of the two sites, of Creag na Caillich or Ruigh Aiteachan, came first for her attention is difficult to determine. Charles Mathew's description of the Huts clearly paints a picture of Creag na Caillich in 1833, but Charles Tankerville's account of his visit also in 1833, seems to describe Ruigh Aiteachan. A settlement already existed at Ruigh Aiteachan before 1830 and it is probable that Georgina extended it by building "the Huts", hence the two groups of buildings. Ruigh Aiteachan would have provided more comfort but Georgina undoubtedly had experience of summer shielings and, in the knowledge that Glen Feshie had been known as "the summer shielings of Dalnavert" in the not too distant past, she perhaps wanted to recreate the shieling life for her guests at Creag na Caillich. Perhaps Creag na Caillich was used for picnicking or the occasional overnight camp, when the parties would have enacted the "shieling style" of life.

## 10. Kinrara – a "humble farmstead" and the inspiration for the settlement in Glen Feshie

There seems no doubt that the early Highland life of Georgina, Duchess of Bedford, had a significant impact upon her. She was born at Gordon Castle, near Fochabers, in Banffshire, the youngest of Jane, Duchess of Gordon's five daughters and was to spend some of her teenage life at Kinrara, her mother's Highland retreat near Aviemore. Duchess Georgina had a great affection for the Highlands and, as we have seen in previous chapters, maintained the association with the Badenoch area by renting the Doune of Rothiemurchus and also the shooting lease in Glen Feshie. Kinrara and her experiences there seem to have been the inspiration for the settlement that she established in Glen Feshie and for the hospitality that she gave her guests.

Jane Maxwell (1749-1812), Georgina's mother, was an intelligent and beautiful woman who in 1767, at the age of 17, married Alexander, 4th Duke of Gordon. The pair had two sons and five daughters, but the marriage was not a happy one, and from the late 1780s the Duke and Duchess were living apart; the Duke openly keeping his mistress, Jane Christie, and their ever growing family at Gordon Castle. It is not known when Duchess Jane first visited Kinrara but Charles Fraser Mackintosh records that in the early part of her marriage she much preferred Kinrara to Gordon Castle:

> She *(Duchess Jane)* was not taken with Gordon Castle but so much struck with Kinrara that she at once made up her mind that it should become a Highland residence..... Both Kinraras *(North and South/Inshriach)* are beautiful and nowhere in Badenoch are the hills so set off with birch than at North Kinrara. But, alas, at the beginning the Duchess's wishes were carried out by the removal of a numerous and contented people.....On 20th February 1770 the Duke sign*(ed)*, in London, a precept agreeable to the ancient Scottish form, to warn out Patrick Grant of Rothiemurchus, principal tenant, and the following people in the personal occupation of the lands of Kinrara and Dellifour; Donald Grant, Peter Grant of Easter Kinrara, John Grant there, John Shaw there, James Grant of Wester Kinrara, Anna Forbes there ....... probably over one hundred souls, doubtless poor enough, but honestly paying the whole rent exacted by the Gordons.........Retiring from the great metropolis (in the 1790s) the Duchess steadily and for long periods lived at Kinrara nearly always accompanied by her daughter Georgina. Lady Georgina was passionately attached to Badenoch. (Fraser Mackintosh, 1897)

An old farmhouse was to become Duchess Jane's summer residence in the 1790s until Kinrara House was built in 1804.

The settlements cleared of their people in the document above are marked on the Roy map of c1750 and also on an estate plan of 1771 and Kinrara-na-belly is in the position of the farmstead thought to have been occupied by Duchess Jane. During the years that followed she developed the estate into a country retreat by designing a picturesque landscape and planting numerous trees taking inspiration from the fashionable landscapers of the day. The trees have matured over the years but today this landscape is largely unchanged.

Several contemporary accounts of Duchess Jane's activities at the old farmhouse exist. Elizabeth Grant in about 1804 says:

> She had for the last few years spent her summers at a little farm on the Badenoch property, a couple of miles higher up the Spey than our Doune, and on the opposite side of the water. She inhabited the real old farmhouse of Kinrara, where she was happier and more agreeable and the society she gathered round her far pleasanter, than it ever was afterwards in the new cottage villa she built a mile nearer to us (Grant, 1898).

Anne Grant of Laggan records:

> The Duchess of Gordon is a very busy farmeress at Kinrara, her beautiful retreat on the Spey. She rises at five in the morning, bustles incessantly, employs from 20 to 30 workmen every day and entertains noble travellers from England in a house very little better than our own, but she is setting up a wooden pavilion to see company in (Grant of Laggan, 1798)

And John Stoddart who was a guest of the Duchess in 1800:

> In this spot, on a knoll commanding the small plain stands the cottage of her Grace, the Duchess of Gordon. The house was a mere Highland farm, no better than others of this country. Her Grace has taken it as it stood, its thatched roof, its outhouses, its barn and byre and with the addition of a single room and with some alteration and arrangement in the others has converted it into a summer residence. The want of coal was supplied by a large peat stack; no baker being to hand, our bread was brought either from Inverness or from Perth by the daily carriages on the road. Add to this that the house itself was by no means well built and the construction of the chimneys so faulty as to fill the rooms frequently with smoke. For the cottage itself some architectural embellishment would be necessary. The Duchess has therefore received several designs for this purpose, but her taste is too correct to adopt any whose simplicity does not accord with the surrounding scenery (Stoddart, 1801).

Elizabeth Grant describes the hospitality given to the Duchess's guests:

> It was a sort of backwoods life, charming to young people amid such scenery, a dramatick emancipation from the forms of society that for a while every season was delightful, particularly as there was no real roughing it. In the but and ben, constituting the small farm cabin she and her daughter, the Lady Georgina, dwelt and with the help of white calico, a little white wash, a little paint and plenty of flowers they made their apartment quite pretty. What had been a kitchen at one end of the house was elevated by various contrivances into a sitting room; a barn was fitted up as a barrack for ladies, stable for gentlemen; a kitchen was formed out of some of the out offices, and in it, without his battery, without his stove, without his thousand and one assistants and resources, her French cook sent up dinners still talked of by the few remaining partakers. The entrees were all prepared in one black

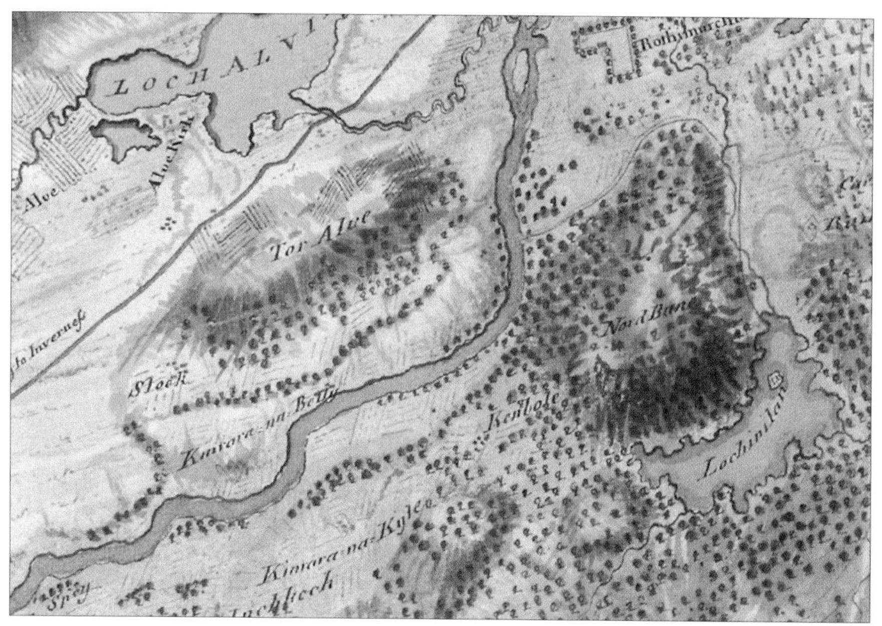


Roy Military map, c1750 of Kinrara and Tor Alvie - © The British Library Board/SCRAN

An etching of the old farmhouse at North Kinrara from Stoddarts book of 1801

> pot - a large potato cauldron, which he had ingeniously divided within into four compartments by means of two pieces of tin sheet crossed, the only inconvenience of this clever plan being that the company had to put up with all white sauces one day and all brown the next. Her favourite footman, Lang James, a very handsome impudent person, but an excellent servant for that sort of wild life, able to put his hand to any work, played the violin remarkably well, and as every tenth Highlander plays on the same instrument tolerably, there was no difficulty in getting up a highly satisfactory band on any evening that the guests were disposed to dancing. Half the London world of fashion, all the clever people that could be hunted out from all parts, all the north country, all the neighbourhood from far and near without regard to wealth or station, and all the kith and kin both of Gordons and Maxwells flocked to this encampment in the wilderness during the fine autumns to enjoy the free life, the pure air, and the wit and fun the Duchess brought with her to the mountains.
> Lady Georgina Gordon the youngest of the fair sisters and the only one unmarried was much liked; all through her life she has shown herself to be kindhearted, in her early youth she was quiet and pleasing as well as lively, so my mother described her when she described those merry doings in the old cottage at Kinrara in the days quite before my memory. Lady Georgina had been some years married to the Duke of Bedford and the Duchess of Gordon was living in her new house in this summer of 1804 when I first recollect them as neighbours. Our two dwellings were little more than a mile apart but the river was between us, a river not always in the mood for assisting intercourse.... But no day passed without a meeting between the Doune and Kinrara. When the Duchess had miscalculated her supplies or more guests arrived than she could possibly accommodate the surplus as a matter of course came over to us. All our spare rooms were often filled and at Kinrara shakedowns in the dining room were resorted to for the gentlemen who were too late for a corner in the wooden "room", a building erected a short way from the house in the midst of a birch thicket....We joined in the fun of this gay summer, we were often over at Kinrara, the Duchess having perpetual dances (Grant, 1898)

During the winter seasons Duchess Jane lived at her London house in Pall Mall. She was a spirited figure who was prominent in social and political society and formed a social centrepiece for the Tory party. When she died in 1812 her body was taken north to be buried at the old Celtic chapel of St Eata at Kinrara where her husband carried out her final wish by erecting a memorial. Duchess Jane's memorial cairn lies in a wood just a short distance from the site of the old farmhouse.

Today the remains of the old farmhouse are seen on a close cropped grassy knoll about one kilometre to the SW of the present Kinrara house. The site has an elevated position above the river and extensive views towards the Cairngorm Mountains. There is evidence of five buildings; the larger two are on the summit of the knoll and the others are seen as platforms which would have held timber structures. The rotting stumps of several mature deciduous trees are seen throughout the site; local information has it that these

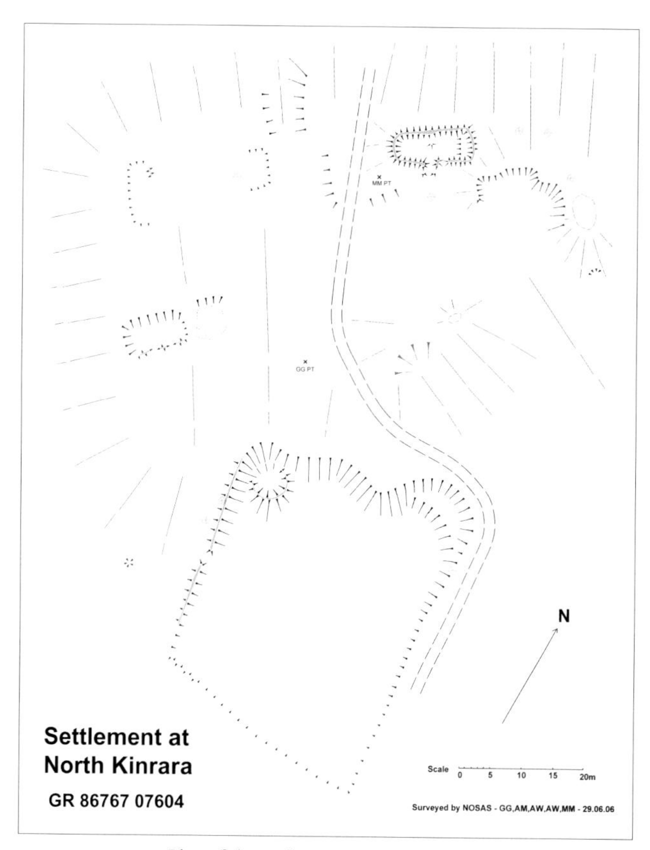


Plan of the settlement at North Kinrara

were wych elm trees, a variety of tree that is not indigenous to these parts. The evidence for this site being that of Duchess Janes' original farmhouse is arguably overwhelming.

The site more or less fits the location described by Elizabeth Grant as "a little farm on the Badenoch property, a couple of miles higher up the Spey than our Doune, and on the opposite side of the water"; the distance between the two sites is exactly that. Elizabeth Grant describes Kinrara House as being just one mile nearer to Doune than the old farmhouse: it is actually 1km nearer, hardly a difference to quibble about. The buildings are of modest size and the wall footings are of turf and stone, typical of an 18th century farmstead; they concur with Stoddarts description "The house was a mere Highland farm, no better than others of this country. Her Grace has taken it as it stood, its thatched roof, its outhouses, its barn and byre".

The settlement is in the position of Kinrara-na-Belly on the Roy map of c1750. An estate plan of 1771 (NAS GD2497), has a farmstead named Kinrara in the same location. Situated on a knoll, this settlement has nine buildings in the same alignment as the footings seen today. The very existence today of settlement remains in an area which has received intensive agricultural activity and landscape design, as this has, is unusual and suggests that the site was respected; it was of value to someone and its preservation was important to them.

The 1801 etching in Stoddarts book has the farmhouse in a commanding position on the summit of a knoll with impressive panoramic views towards the Cairngorm Mountains. The aspect, topography and view towards the mountains more or less match the site of the farmstead, although the sketch shows the countryside as much more open, not surprising since many of the trees would not have been planted then. The two main buildings in the sketch have an appropriate relationship to one another. The building on the left may be that marked on the estate plan of 1771; today this site is in a field which is regularly ploughed and all evidence of it has been destroyed. The other 3 buildings which were recorded as platforms at the site and the wych elm trees are not seen on the sketch, possibly because they were not in existence at this early stage or possibly because the artist, or indeed the Duchess, preferred to omit them from the picturesque landscape; she wished to maintain this simple farmhouse in its surrounding scenery. According to Stoddart "the Duchess' taste is too correct to adopt any "designs for embellishment to the farmhouse" whose simplicity does not accord with the surrounding scenery", this may explain why, when she came to build Kinrara House only a couple of years later, she chose its present situation well away from the farmhouse.

Duchess Jane requested that, when she died, her remains should be buried at the site of St Eatas chapel; the memorial cairn lies in the trees on the left of the Stoddart sketch, just a few hundred metres away from the old farmhouse.

Duchess Georgina was to lease Elizabeth Grants old home of the Doune of Rothiemurchus for her autumn sojourns, establishing her own settlement in Glen Feshie where she lived a fairytale existence introducing her guests to the "rough" life of the Highlands and entertaining them in a similar manner to that which her mother had done at Kinrara. Duchess Jane's husband, the 4th Duke of Gordon, died in 1827 and the Gordon Estates, including Kinrara, passed to George, 5th Duke of Gordon, Duchess Georginas' brother.

## 11. Glen Feshie in the late 19th and the 20th Centuries

The MacPherson-Grants continued to own the Invereshie part of Glen Feshie in the latter part of the 19th century and in addition leased the east side of the glen from "the Mackintosh", bringing both sides of the river together into one estate. It was to be 1925 before the east side of the river was purchased. Shooting tenants paid increasing sums to lease the deer forest and the grouse moors. The Duke of Leeds has already been mentioned as tenanting the estate in the 1850s; Sir John Ramsden, Sir Charles Maurdant, Baron Schroeder and the Right Honourable Edward Horsman were some of the others in the following decades. Improvements and refinements were made during this period; access to the hills was facilitated by the construction of stalkers tracks and bridges and a completely new lodge, the present Glenfeshie Lodge, was built in 1892. Glen Feshie continued into the 1900s as a most desirable sporting estate and provided employment for a good number of keepers and ghillies. But the large population numbers of the "Duchess of Bedford" days were to drop considerably over the latter half of the 19th century. In Glen Feshie alone 16 households comprising 44 adults and 30 children were recorded in the census of 1861 but by 1871 this had reduced to 8 households with 24 adults and 11 children and in 1901 there were 18 adults and 10 children with several buildings noted as being uninhabited.

### Schooling in Glen Feshie

Since the time of the Reformation parish schools had been deeply embedded in Scottish rural society with landowners required to make a contribution towards the building of a schoolhouse and the salary of a teacher. Education was not compulsory until the Education Act of 1872, but kirk sessions often paid the fees of poorer children and by the 19th century the parish schools were supplemented by a variety of other schools. Christian organisations were to make a significant contribution to education seeing the Highlands as missionary territory, but nevertheless education in the Highlands was patchy and in 1792 the OSA for Kingussie records that the provision of schooling in the parish was poor:

> *(there is in the parish)* one parochial school with number of scholars varying from 20 to 50. This is owing to the children of the tenantry being sent to attend the cattle in the hills during the summer months. Parents are often unable to afford the expense of giving their children even the common education, and the greater number of them are so illiterate that they can neither read nor write

By 1835 the situation has improved and the NSA reports:

> The number of young people betwixt 6 and 15 years of age who cannot read or write amounts to about 39. The schools are obviously producing a very beneficial effect.

There is evidence that the large number of children in Glen Feshie received some sort of schooling at this time. In 1841 when the 12 year old William Collie was living at Carnachuin he tells us:

> I was badly situated for school. There was a parochial school open during the

winter 3 or 4 miles away and during the winter of 1843-44 when living at Dalnavert I attended the Laganlia School where we had an excellent teacher (Collie, 1908)

Dr Alexander Cameron (1827 – 1885), who later in his life was to become a respected scholar of Gaelic Literature, spent some of his early days as a teacher in Glen Feshie. Born at Torcroy, near Kingussie and brought up at Druimguish, his experiences as a schoolteacher in Glenfeshie in about 1844 at the age of 17 are related by his biographers:

He *(Alexander Cameron)* attended school in Kingussie and proved to be a very able scholar; he also for a short time attended the school at Insh, where he probably got his first smattering of Latin. He then returned to his former teacher *(in Kingussie)*, who was a somewhat strict disciplinarian, but who seems to have taken kindly to his promising pupil and to have encouraged him in every possible manner. Mr Cameron had by this time made such progress as to be deemed fit to conduct a side school at Glenfeshie, when, as he thought himself, he was hardly fit to teach, but rather required to be taught..... There are not a few of his old pupils still living who have testified to the unusual amount of painstaking labour he bestowed upon them, many of them were far older and taller than their teacher. It was the general habit then for lads and others beyond their 'teens" to work manually in summer and attend school during the quiet winter months. His short term of teaching in this then somewhat solitary, though well-peopled glen, earned for him a reputation for thoroughness in work and good discipline that has not yet ceased to be talked about (MacBain and Kennedy, 1892)

Today it is generally known that the building at Stronetoper was a schoolhouse, but what is not so clear is when it was built. In 1872 the Education Act required all children to attend school, but the need for a school in Glen Feshie was recognised before this. In 1865 Georgina MacPherson-Grant wrote to her nephew, George Macpherson-Grant of Ballindalloch, offering to part fund a schoolhouse and the salary for a schoolmaster in the glen (NRAS 771/Bundle 105). Plans for the school and schoolmasters house were drawn up in 1866 and the school appears to have been completed by 1869 when two roofed buildings are marked on the 1st edition OS map. The school has taken its name from the settlement of Stronantobhair, 600m to the south, where a single unroofed building is marked on the 1st edition OS map. The census records from 1881 to 1901 have the Stronetoper schoolhouse as uninhabited but in 1901 Malcolm Macpherson, described as a teacher, is living with his brother, a gamekeeper, at Achleum lodge, across the river.

Between 1928 and 1947 the Glenfeshie school log book records several occasions when the children from further afield could not attend school because of snow drifts or flooded streams and on some occasions they were kept at home to help with the planting. By 1939 there were 14 children attending and by 1943 only 4; the school was closed in 1947. An elderly lady, who for the purposes of this account will be called Janet, has memories of a childhood in the glen in the 1930s. The family initially leased the schoolhouse at Stronetoper during the summer months but later, during WW2, they lived more permanently lower down the glen at Balachroick. Janet attended the school at Stronetoper and in her teens was to go to the secondary school in Kingussie:

> I went from Balachroick on my bike - 14 miles, there was no other way of doing it. I used to be terrified when it was dark. I joined a girl from the post office at Feshie Bridge and we used to cycle into Kingussie. Then a road and a bridge were built by the Canadians, to get the timber across the river just below us. It shortened the journey and we went by Drumguish and over to Kingussie. We used to cycle that way to church and to go to the pictures.

**WW2 and Military training**

During the Second World War Glen Feshie and the Lodge were requisitioned and used for military training. Initially there were two camps and the training was principally in skiing and mountain warfare. Later, in 1943, the "Highland Fieldcraft Training Centre" was set up by Lieutenant-Colonel TGP Corbett, 2nd Baron Rowallan, an officer with experience of adventure training both in military and civilian life. The training was directed towards potential officers, and activities were designed to build responsibility, confidence and ability to work with others. They were run along "Outward Bound" lines and aimed at developing the whole person rather than just his physique; the claim in short, was "to make men out of boys".

The Mountain and Snow Warfare School was ejected from Glenfeshie Lodge to make way for the new training centre's headquarters and officer's mess. Two camps were established, one formerly used by the Mountain Warfare School and the other a vacant hutted camp built for the Canadian Forestry Corps. Each course ran for 10 weeks and the first intake in May 1943 had 120 students. The courses covered a huge range of activities which included weapons training, fieldcraft, navigation and signalling, weather forecasting and botany, hill walking and bivouacking in the hills, river crossing, rope bridge building, rock climbing, rafting, tree felling, endurance exercises, unarmed combat and many more. The location of Glen Feshie was ideal for most of the year but the courses did not include skiing or winter warfare so, to escape the snows that blocked the access roads to the glen, winter quarters were centred on the village of Poolewe in Wester Ross.

The courses were deemed to be successful and Lord Rowallan later recounted the comment of the Selection Board Chairman "You may have succeeded in producing 80 per cent of officers, but more importantly, you have produced 100 per cent of men". Even for those students who did not pass there was a feeling that the experience and their efforts had not been wasted. As one successful student put it the purpose of the course was "making 18 year olds into 22 year olds in ten weeks. (Allan 2007)

Janet has memories of the military training in the glen during WW2:

> We were never aware of the firing because we were lower down the glen at Balachroick, but sometime if we were going up for a picnic we were

Assault course at the Highland Fieldcraft Training Centre Glenfeshie, 1944 -
© National Museums Scotland (M.2003.7)

> stopped.......we were regarded as residents, nobody queried whether we were there or not, and we knew that there were mountain training people further up - there were two camps at the top of the glen. We were told, probably by them, that they were training for D day, by others that they were training for Norway. The top lot was Lord Rowallans bunch who were highly trained mountain soldiers - elite SAS type troops. They were in a camp near the top pony bridge *(at Carnachuin)*, there was a big camp on a grassy area. There were Norwegians training in Glen Feshie too, it was absolutely hotching with troops......*(the ropeway)* was a block and tackle affair, for all the world like a bucket on a string, just below and north of the kennels on a very steep bit of the bank. These poor guys used to have to go across from the kennel side of the river to the other side, at the double. They had to go over and across the moor to the corrie burn, Corrie Garbhalach, up the hill, Sgoran Dubh, and back again before breakfast - every day.

The centre closed in November 1944 and the experiences gained by the officers and men who attended the courses was such that an association was set up after the war, not unusual for service organizations where men who had served and fought together in the war were concerned, but unusual for such a short lived organization. A monument on a small knoll at Carnachuin has the inscription "Highland Fieldcraft Training Centre -

1943-1945 – In memory of those who gave their lives for their country and who trained in this glen and at Gairloch, Ross-shire".

Physical remains of wartime training are still seen in the glen today. On a terrace to the north of Carnachuin are the concrete platforms of the Nissen huts and in the wood of Coille an Torr, on the east side of the river, there are complex remains of trenches, platforms, scoops, gun sites and water tanks.

**Timber exploitation during wartime**

The Forestry Commission was established in the years following the First World War (1914-18) with the remit of replenishing the timber that had been felled during the war, but the trees which were planted were not sufficiently mature by the time of the Second World War. Private land owners were once again called upon to provide timber for the war effort. In Glen Feshie the Canadian Forestry Corps were mobilized to do the felling:

> They brought with them the most up-to-date logging equipment then available in Canada: caterpillar tractors for extracting the timber, fast diesel powered saw benches, winches for high lead logging and bull-dozers for road building (Smout 2003).

Janet tells us:

> The next thing was the arrival of the Canadian Timber Corp. They were part of the Canadian Army, and had a training role and a timber role. There were two or three camps and they were training for mountain warfare and doing the timber work at the same time...They were taking the trees down off the face of the hill behind Balachroick on the steep slopes. But first of all they had to make a roadway down from the trees across the river and to the timber camp, which was on the Corarnstil side of the river, at Tolvah. They made a very good road from the Red Burn just north of us, over to the saw mill at Tolvah and the bridge was quite substantial. The wood was transported down the glen on lorries....they *(the loggers)* were very generous, we were just early teenagers at the time and we thought it was just wonderful to be invited to the ENSA concerts. If ever there was an ENSA concert we were all invited over. We used to go over the bridge and then later on we were invited to the dances in Insh Hall - "Paraffin palley" as we knew it. I can remember the unpolished floor, with knots literally this size (3") and the paraffin lamps hanging from the roof. The soldiers had tackity boots and they all learned the Scottish reels. It was understood that if you went for a dance with someone, they took you for tea afterwards and you were given a plateful of sandwiches, scones and pancakes and it was the height of rudeness if you didn't eat them.

Another elderly gentleman was at school in Kingussie at the time; he talks about being invited to picnics organised by the Canadian Forestry Corp at the camp on Sunday afternoons too. He said they felt very privileged to be invited to a day of sports and picnic at the camp.

Aerial photographs of 1946 reveal evidence of extensive felling in the glen, particularly on the east side of the river. Extraction tracks are seen throughout the glen and to the north of Carnachuin there is a bridge and a saw mill, with a large camp and a further saw mill at Tolvah. Frank Fraser Darling, naturalist and author, describes the destruction in 1949:

> Our land is so devastated that we might as well have been in a battlefield. See the very windbreaks taken from the roadsides, see the wreck of Glenfeshie and Rothiemurchus that is no more.

In the years that followed the war indiscriminate planting of trees to replenish stocks of timber was to take place throughout the Highlands and in the 1960s and 70s a patchwork of conifer plantations with ugly bulldozed tracks appeared in Glen Feshie. In 1967 Macpherson Grant of Ballindaloch sold the estate to Lord Dulverton, and it then passed to John Dibben who was followed by the Wills Woodland Trust. Some of these private hands were insensitive in their actions and plans for development, but such was the outcry from the conservationists, who recognised the significance of the natural heritage of the glen, that many of the proposals had to be significantly reduced. Interest in the estate was shown by bodies such as The John Muir Trust, the RSPB and the National Trust for Scotland but the glen has remained in private hands.

**The Future**

For the last 15 years the Glenfeshie Estate has been owned by a succession of Danish Industrialists. The first of these was Flemming Skouboe who made significant improvements to the infrastructure of the estate, upgrading the lodge and employee's accommodation and improving the access road up the glen. Since 2001 the policy of management towards the natural heritage has been much more sensitive with regard to conserving and sustaining the natural heritage. The present owner, Anders Holch Poulsen, has the objective of holding the deer population low in order to allow the land to regain its ecological potential. This will allow the Caledonian Pine woods to become re-established, and also the arctic and sub-alpine habitats with their associated plant communities. Scottish Natural Heritage and the Cairngorm National Park Authority are aware of this policy and fully support it. The future for the natural and cultural heritage of Glen Feshie looks bright and hopefully we will be able to enjoy it for many years to come.

## Bibliography


Allan, Stuart (2007) - *Commando Country*

Anderson, RD (1997) *Scottish Education since the Reformation: Studies in Scottish Economic and Social History No 5*

Baird, Rosemary - *Mistress of the House – Great ladies and Grand houses 1670 – 1830*

Bil, A *(1990) - The Shieling 1600-1840*

Census Records - *1841 to 1901*

Collie, William (1908) - *Memoirs of William Collie: A 19th Century Deerstalker*

Dickens, C (editor) (1879) - *Life of Charles Mathews*

Devine, Tom (2006) - *Clearance and Improvement: Land. Power and People in Scotland 1700 to 1900*

Fenton, A. (1976) revised 1999 - *Scottish Country Life*

Fraser Mackintosh, C (1897) - *Antiquarian Notes*

Fraser Mackintosh, C (1898) - *Minor Septs of Clan Chattan*

Gordon Margaret (1870) - *The Home Life of Sir David Brewster*

Grant of Laggan, Anne (1798) – *Letters from the Mountains*

Grant, Elizabeth (1898) reprinted 1988 - *Memoirs of a Highland Lady*

Grimble, Augustus (1901) - *Deer Stalking and Deer Forests of Scotland*

Haldane, ARB (1997) - *The Drove Roads of Scotland*

Helps, Arthur (Ed) (1868) – *Leaves from the Journal of Our Life in The Highlands*

Historic Scotland (1988) - *An Inventory of Gardens and Designed Landscapes, Volume 2, Highlands and Islands*

Lennie, Campbell (1976) - *Landseer, The Victorian Paragon*

MacBain, Alexander and Kennedy, Rev. John (editors) (1892) – *Reliquiae Celtica (Vol 1 Ossianica): Texts Papers and Studies in Gaelic Literature and Philology left by the late Rev. Alexander Cameron*

Murray of Kensington, Sarah (1799) - *A Companion and Useful Guide to the Beauties of Scotland*

National Archives of Scotland - *GD44 Papers of the Gordon Family*

National Archives of Scotland - *GD176 Mackintosh Papers*

National Archives of Scotland - *GD128 Fraser Mackintosh Papers*

National Register of Archives Scotland - *NRAS771 Papers of the Macpherson Grant Family of Ballindalloch*

*New Statistical Account for Parishes of Kingussie, Insh and Alvie, 1835*

*Old Statistical Account for Parishes of Kingussie, Insh and Alvie, 1791-1799*

Ormond, R. (2005) - *The Monarch of the Glen - Landseer in the Highlands*

RCAHMS (1995) - *Mar Lodge Estate - An Archaeological Survey,*

Russell, Helen (1995) - *The Past Around Us*

Scarlett, Meta Humphrey (1988) - *In the Glens Where I Was Young*

Scrope, W (1883) - *Days of Deer Stalking in the Scottish Highlands*

Smout, TC (1999) - *Rothiemurchus, Nature and People on a Highland Estate*

Smout, TC (2003) - *People and Woods in Scotland, A History*

Sommers, Robert (1848) – *Letters from the Highlands (After the Great Potato Famine of 1846)*

Stoddart, Sir John (1801) - *Remarks on Local Scenery and manners in Scotland during 1799 and 1800*

Tankerville, Charles (1891) - *The Chillingham Wild Cattle, Reminiscences of Life in the Highlands.*

Thornton, Col Thomas (1804) - *Tour through the Highlands and the North of England*

Trethewey, Rachel (2002) - *Mistress of the Arts - The Passionate life of Georgina. Duchess of Bedford*